FIGHTER
OPERATIONS

Patrick Stephens Limited, a member of the Haynes Publishing Group, has published authoritative, quality books for enthusiasts for a quarter of a century. During that time the company has established a reputation as one of the world's leading publishers of books on aviation, maritime, military, model-making, motor cycling, motoring, motor racing, railway and railway modelling subjects. Readers or authors with suggestions for books they would like to see published are invited to write to: The Editorial Director, Patrick Stephens Limited, Sparkford, Nr Yeovil, Somerset, BA22 7JJ.

FIGHTER OPERATIONS

The tactics and techniques of air combat, from World War I to the Gulf War

JERRY SCUTTS

Patrick Stephens Limited

First published in 1992

British Library Cataloguing in Publication Data
A catalogue record for this book is available from the British Library.

ISBN 1 85260 127 2

Library of Congress Cataloging in Publication No. 92-81443

Patrick Stephens Limited is part of the Haynes Publishing Group P.L.C., Sparkford, Nr Yeovil, Somerset, BA22 7JJ.

Printed by Redwood Press Limited, Melksham, Wilts

Contents

Acknowledgement

In compiling this record of fighter combat I would like particularly to thank Gary Nelson and Stuart Leslie, Andy Bunce of British Aerospace, RAF Strike Command Headquarters, Howard Tanner, Douglas Reese, Glenn McCorkle and Arden Gibson.

Introduction

For 78 years the world's air forces have used fighter aircraft to establish and maintain air superiority and to enable ground forces, naval fleets or other air assets to prosecute tactical or strategic operations in wartime with a degree of immunity from enemy air attack. Whatever the fighter has been called over the years—scout, pursuit or interceptor—the basic operational requirement has remained unchanged. In addition, the fighter has had an important defensive role against bombers, ground attack aircraft in various categories, and other fighters.

Ever since the first scout aeroplanes of opposing sides met and challenged each other using rudimentary hand-held weapons in the early months of the First World War, fighters have formed an integral part of air arms of any size. As the first air war developed into a gruelling contest in which each side sought to maintain a degree of freedom to conduct observation and bombing sorties, so fighter protection became of paramount importance. Young men, trained in Army methods, volunteered for pilot and observer duties and thereby opened a new chapter in warfare.

There were few manuals on such a new method of fighting. Aeroplanes themselves were in their infancy, and to many eyes they seemed extraordinarily dangerous devices, but, whatever the risks, airmen regarded the war in the air as a more civilized activity than the bloody carnage that developed on the ground as 19th-century battlefield doctrine met 20th-century weapons.

Scout pilots also captured the imagination of the general public, as their exploits received due publicity in the press. In the days when advances of a few yards on the Western Front were measured in hundreds, if not thousands of corpses, air combat was one of the few military activities in which the individual could still shine and stand by his demonstrable prowess. Men who shot down aircraft of the opposing side in substantial numbers became national heroes. Although the reality behind the 'thrilling exploits' journalese of the Press was often far less romantic, such men became the modern embodiment of the knights and crusaders of the past.

It was the French who first coined the term 'ace' to denote a pilot who destroyed five enemy aircraft in aerial combat, and, ever since, this yardstick has been a convenient way to distinguish the most skilful fighter pilots from the rank and file. During World War One numerous individuals won their spurs and became outstanding aces by hunting alone, relying solely on their own ability to find enemy aircraft and to shoot them down. Gradually, owing to the increasing number of aeroplanes deployed, this became so risky an occupation that the 'lone wolf' became an anachronism—indeed, the very survival of a mutually-protective fighter formation could be placed in jeopardy by such tactics, and it was regarded as foolhardy if one man sacrificed the element of surprise by making his move too soon. It continued to happen, but tactical considerations generally required fighter formations to stay together and split up only when combat was joined.

When, on 11 November 1918, the Armistice brought World War One to an end, most of the lessons that had been learned about air fighting were at best shelved and at worst forgotten. It was to be an extreme irony that Germany, which was in no position to put any such lessons into practice for another 18 years, possibly remembered more of the fundamentals of air fighting than did the victorious Allies when arms were taken up again in 1939. By then many members of the *Luftwaffe* had been in action during the Spanish Civil War, and few learned so much about the inherent advantages of modern enclosed-cockpit monoplane fighters than the embryo *Jagdflieger*.

So strident was the late 1918 call for 'swords into ploughshares', that not only were the instruments of war destroyed *en masse*, but the textbooks and, indeed, the ideas, seemingly went on the bonfires as well. By the early 1920s the 'war to end wars' had succeeded in removing all but a very modest air defence force from the military inventories of Britain and France, the two major Allied powers.

The years of peace between the wars also saw a general slowing down of research and development, so that, for example, the advantage of the monoplane over the traditional biplane was slow in being realised. As far as the single-seat fighter was concerned, the first-line equipment of the 1930s differed little externally from the machines that had fought the Great War. Close comparison of the performance of aircraft from each era reveals that ten years of aeronautical development had given the Hawker Fury 8,500 ft more ceiling than the S.E.5a and about an extra 80 m.p.h. in top speed, and the number of guns, two, was exactly the same. Although the Fury was a fine aircraft, and the RAF's foremost interceptor of between 1931 and 1939, a cynic might have been moved to suggest that the desire for a lasting peace was being taken far too much for granted.

Just as the fighters themselves had undergone little radical change, so the way they were deployed, particularly by the Royal Air Force, hardly progressed at all. The old First World War 'Vic' formations so appreciated by air display crowds were still in vogue as operational doctrine. Worst of all, perhaps, was the fact that bombers of the period were almost as fast as the interceptors that would have been pitted against them in a future conflict.

It was not, therefore, surprising that the inter-war years put relatively little strain on the profession of fighter pilot. While many men became highly experienced pilots (only the Russians were to take the giant step of introducing the fairer sex to the art of air combat), ways of deploying fighters effectively remained vague and ill-defined.

The inter-war period saw great international emphasis laid on the role of the bomber. Just as a later generation of military planners were to believe (for a mercifully short period) that the manned fighter could do little in a miltary scenario overshadowed by guided missiles, so the 'thirties were dominated by the assumption that bombers, irrespective of the strength of fighter and fixed ground defences, were the ultimate instrument of power in the air. This view remained paramount in military circles for some time, certainly into the middle years of World War Two.

Even when a new generation of monoplane fighters had entered service, this lack of understanding of their true potential was to cost many nations dear when Germany, bent on a second try at military domination in Europe, showed how effective a sizeable, properly deployed and well-flown fighter force could be. The rate of loss suffered by the European air arms when Germany launched her attack in the west in May 1940 was staggering. It was exceeded in June 1941, when the *Luftwaffe* smashed into Russia. In both cases, German success was mainly due to one aircraft, the Messerschmitt Bf 109.

On the other side of the world, Japan's military ambitions in Asia also had at their core one excellent fighter. The build-up of a strong naval air striking force was spearheaded by the superlative Mitsubishi A6M. As it was, of necessity, a long-range fighter, the A6M's designers sacrificed almost all other attributes to light weight and the ability to fly great distances (up to 1,930 miles), and the deadly 'Zero' was as nasty a shock to the Allies in the Far East as the Bf 109 was in Western Europe. These two significantly different fighters gained important psychological as well as military advantages out of all proportion to any technical ascendency they possessed over the fighters of other nations.

'A nasty shock to the Allies.' Due mainly to its phenomenal range, the Mitsubishi A6M Zero-Sen could be flown at speeds as low as 135 m.p.h. with fuel consumption dropping to a miserly 18 gal per hour. A simple but convenient bowser was often all that was necessary to fill the 34 gal fuselage tank of an A6M5. (via Rene Francillon)

In the closing months of World War Two there was little to match the Hawker Tempest, either on the enemy or Allied side. But in common with a considerable number of other high-performance fighters, the Tempest reached operational status after the vast aerial duels that had marked the middle years of the war had ceased. (Hawker)

The Germans and Japanese were amazed at how quickly the force of their arms won the day against countries which had, for various reasons, neglected to modernise their military forces, and in particular their means of adequate defence in the air. Combat again elevated *Luftwaffe* fighter pilots to the status of national heroes, who had been instrumental in destroying the enemy's will and means to fight.

Fighters proliferated as land- and carrier-based weapons, their role changing from that of short-range 'area defence', a primary example of which was the RAF's success in the Battle of Britain, to a remarkably efficient tactical offensive instrument which was being exploited to the full by 1944. Under the impetus of war, single-seat—and often single-engined—fighters earned a reputation second to none for their ability to make the difference between victory and defeat in innumerable localised battles.

Developed into devastating ground-attack weapons, able to operate at hitherto undreamed of ranges from their bases, fighters also offered a remark-ably high return on investment compared with multi-crew bombers. No finer examples of the long-range fighter need be cited than the North American Mustang or the de Havilland Mosquito. Again, these two aircraft differed radically, but their ability to carry out the task in hand at a similar maximum range of 1,700 miles with external fuel tanks was never bettered.

When it came to the shorter-range types, the Spitfire, Tempest and Fw 190 had few equals at different periods of the war when, particularly in the case of the German type, the standard of pilot training and availability of fuel were significant factors. In the fighter-bomber stakes, the Fw 190, P-47 and Typhoon must be high on any list of the 'top ten' types, but, as the nature of the war changed, few fighters were destined to remain pure interceptors.

Almost without exception, all of the combatant powers were obliged to hang range-boosting fuel tanks, bombs and rockets on fighters in order to support ground forces or to harass enemy columns, vehicles and shipping, as well as to attack fixed structures of all kinds. These practices were often instrumental in bringing campaigns and, ultimately, the war itself, to a speedy conclusion.

Among those nations that had developed a variety of aircraft types for specialised roles and were in a position to field the necessary numbers so that fighters could continue to combat the enemy in the air was Russia. There, as in the USA, the industrial resources to build aircraft in vast numbers worked through to victory on the battlefield. Masters of the lower-altitude dogfighting environment, the pilots of the Red Air Force's Yak-9s and La-7s generally flew without the encumbrance of ground-attack weapons.

By 1945 the wheel had turned full circle. In Europe the *Luftwaffe*'s attrition rate far exceeded anything that the Germans themselves had meted out in 1940. Despite the continuing high quality of the hardware, which was rarely in short supply despite the bomb tonnage dropped on airfields, supply centres and production lines, the Germans were worn down by the sheer scale of their chosen fighting fronts and the size of the enemy ranged against them, particularly in terms of fighter forces. A further highly significant consideration forced upon the Axis powers was the dwindling supply of aviation fuel and oil.

How a nation deployed its fighter force at any given time depended on the prevailing strategic and tactical conditions. In Western Europe, the ongoing need for heavy bomber escort generally saw the P-51 concentrating on that role, coupled with ground strafing. Often using only fixed guns for this work, North

One of a select few aircraft of the war to be forever associated with a particular type of weapon, the Hawker Typhoon was synonymous with the rocket projectile. At no small risk to themselves, Typhoon pilots excelled in using this devastating weapon against all types of ground target. Typhoon Mk. I FK497 was used for many of the trial flights to test the rockets.

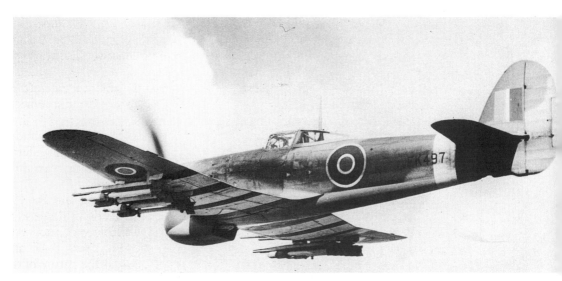

With one of the least mistakable outlines of the war, the Lockheed P-38 Lightning earned a fine reputation throughout the various combat theatres, but in the Pacific its long-range qualities came into their own. This is a P-38L, distinguishable by the port wing landing light. All other models had a retractable light under the wing. (Lockheed)

The vast Pacific ocean provides a fitting backdrop to a Grumman F6F-3 Hellcat of VF-2, photographed on 28 April 1944, when the squadron was embarked aboard the USS Hornet. The parent unit, Air Group Two, was identified in this case by the white spot on the fin. More than any other fighter, the F6F was responsible for the US Navy's final victory over the Japanese. (National Archives)

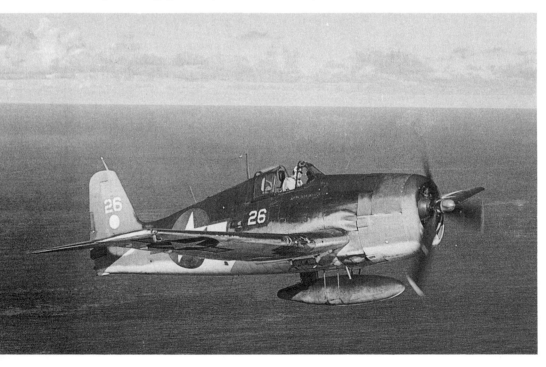

The other arm of the main 'one-two' late-war US Navy carrier fighter punch (not forgetting that the Wildcat was still pitching in) was the mighty Vought F4U Corsair. Extensively used by Marine Corps squadrons from land bases, as well as from carriers, the F4U was rightly regarded as one of the best fighters of the war. These machines are part of the 4th Marine Air Wing escort for Admiral Chester Nimitz's visit to Iwo Jima in March 1945. (USMC)

American's fighter carried out its share of ground-attack operations with bombs and rockets in this and all other war theatres.

Conditions were fundamentally different in the Pacific, where the distances between bases and targets determined how aircraft were deployed. Only towards the end of the war, when the Japanese home islands were in range of Allied airfields, did the AAF deploy a large escort force, and then only for a short time. One type in particular, the P-38 Lightning, exemplified the long-range 'all duties' demands of the island-hopping war as far as the Army was concerned. The other arm of the 'one-two' punch against the Japanese was the US Navy carrier fighter force. An integral part of each task force was the screen of F6F Hellcats and F4U Corsairs, whose primary tasks were to defend the fleet against enemy air attack and to escort dive and strike bombers.

As Japan's fortunes waned, so she, like Germany, suffered a degradation of pilot training standards, along with crippling attrition and a loss of oil supplies that was to prove decisive even before the notorious *Kamikaze* programme made any conventional fighter combat comparisons all but irrelevant. Producing more first-line fighter types than other combatant powers, Japan's designers strove to combine superb aerobatic qualities—which meant light weight and less armour protection and armament—with an ability to destroy tougher, better armed opponents. Overall, this laudable ideal failed.

Fighter tactics themselves changed out of all recognition. Learning from the enemy was hard, but the lessons were gradually taken on board by nations which had previously thought their own operational plans to be sound enough. Thus the RAF and later the USAAF adopted the *Luftwaffe* 'finger-four' formation to extremely good effect.

In fighter armament, the British rapidly grasped the widely-held European belief in the ability of shell-firing cannon to inflict lethal damage on bombers, compared with light machine guns. The American adoption of a battery of heavy machine guns of a calibre midway between the lighter MG and cannon proved equally sound. All three types of gun, in a wide variety of installations and numbers carried, were found to be highly effective in combat. Gunsights also progressed, from the simplest telescopic devices to the sophisticated reflector 'ace-maker' type.

As the fighter's role widened to meet changing wartime demand, the fighter became an excellent dual-role weapon. In some instances ground attack was vested only in heavy calibre guns, the Germans particularly experimenting with a wide variety. Operationally, the Allies stuck with 'tried and tested' guns of relatively small calibres, although the 40 mm Vickers cannon was successfully used by Hurricanes in the anti-tank role. Mosquitoes packed the big 57 mm Molins gun for attacks on shipping.

In the 'big gun' stakes, the Hurricane was the only British single-engined fighter so equipped to see operational service, although larger-calibre cannon were developed and tested. On the American side the 37 mm weapon fitted to the Bell P-39 Airacobra came close, as did various heavy cannon developed by the Germans. Both sides experimented extensively with heavy guns, although in general these close-range weapons were overtaken by 'stand-off' weapons such as the rocket projectile, which offered far less risk to the attacking aircraft. Depicted with the 40 mm cannon in KZ193, one of two Mk. Vs which were flown with a four-blade airscrew for the ground-boosted Merlin 32 engine.

However, by far the most effective and widely used fighter-bomber weapon was the rocket projectile. Useful against virtually any type of ground target and, in the case of the German R4M, capable of inflicting fatal damage to heavy bombers with very few rounds, the aerial rocket enabled single-engined fighters to attack targets with power likened to that of a naval broadside. It remained a ground-attack weapon in the main because apart from the limited use of the German example mentioned, the necessary guidance systems for air-to-air work had not been developed before the war's end.

When the jet engine became a realistic means of fighter propulsion, other developments, such as the ejector seat and the 'G-suit' came into being. Indeed, the latter was by no means exclusive to jet aircraft; American fighter pilots were using such suits to counter the effects of high-speed manoeuvres in piston-engined fighters some time before the end of the war.

As the size and speed of engaged fighter forces increased, so too did the need for a co-ordinated ground control system to direct fighters to make the most economical use of available numbers. By the end of the war some progress had been made towards airborne control, although, in general, fighters were directed from ground or shipboard stations.

Radar greatly increased the potential of the larger multi-seat fighter with room for a specialised operator, and the success of the night- and bad-weather fighter was spectacular. Small transmitters and receivers adapted for use in single-seat fighters such as the F6F Hellcat and F4U Corsair arguably brought about the ultimate wartime development of this class of aircraft.

By the closing stages of the war, the most significant advances for military aircraft in general and fighters in particular had made their combat debuts. While the advent of a reliable turbojet had to wait until the end of hostilities, the ever-inventive Germans, spurred by increasing desperation, channelled resources into aeronautical research that would save their erstwhile antagonists many years of work.

By the end of World War Two a programme of widespread disarmament was again instigated by the Allies, although a new build-up to the force levels dictated by a vastly different world situation was faster than it had been in 1918. Electronics played an increasingly important role in fighter equipment and deployment in the jet age. Fighters continued to have the invaluable asset of their own radar, and in some war theatres under certain circumstances there was a limited return to 'lone-wolf' tactics, particularly at night.

But, through Korea and the air combat phases of Vietnam, the basic tactical doctrine for day fighters evolved by the Germans in Spain prevailed. After Korea there were many who thought that new aircraft crammed with electronic devices and fighting with missiles rather than guns would need a totally new set of deployment rules. To a large extent they were wrong.

Despite the fact that the jet interceptors of the 1950s and '60s evolved into highly complex 'weapons systems', many fundamental rules were found still to apply. The combat scenario that actually developed was often different to that envisaged when military planners and designers sat down to discuss the 'next generation' of fighters. They had no way of knowing that they were—perhaps understandably in the circumstances of the Cold War—envisaging events that would not actually happen.

To them, in the light of a whole range of weapons that appeared virtually automatic in deployment, it was not the tactics, but the pilot himself who appeared to be outdated. At best he would soon be there merely to monitor his systems.

When seasoned fighter pilots finally got their hands on the sophisticated new fighters with magic weapons, they realised that things only *seemed* to have changed. In combat situations far removed from total world war you still needed a good pair of eyes to see the opponent before he saw you. It rapidly became clear that the old-fashioned dogfight was still the way that opposing fighter forces decided the issue, and that anything approaching 'fire and forget' beyond-visual-range weapons was out. The area of sky needed for a dogfight may have grown to encompass miles rather than thousands of yards, and the speeds at which combats were fought might have increased appreciably since Korea, but a fighter pilot still had to have good positioning to make a kill, even with radar-guided missiles. Human input was still the deciding factor.

In Vietnam, F-4 Phantom crews often bemoaned the fact that their aircraft did not have a gun for close-in attacks when their missiles had been expended or had malfunctioned. In the Falklands conflict Royal Navy Harrier pilots could well have been faced with the opposite situation. While their aircraft had a pair of cannon, a reliable air-to-air missile was needed to extend their kill range, particularly against fast and low 'under-the-radar' anti-shipping strikes. Fortunately, rapid adaptation of the AIM-9L Sidewinder for the Harrier provided that capability for a 'David and Goliath' series of air engagements.

The Falklands proved once again that it is not always numbers that decide the outcome of air combat. It may appear to be vital to have dozens of aircraft, each with a specific job to do, on a single mission, but as the USA found in Vietnam, shooting the enemy down—not a primary task in that war—came down to a small number of aircraft at flight strength or less, often manoeuvring one-on-one. Any field commander would welcome the opportunity to send out a task force rather than a couple of elements to complete an operation, but in the South Atlantic, for example, the number of aircraft deployed in any one combat was never high, simply because they were not available. From the British viewpoint, the outcome hardly reflected this fact.

While Vietnam showed that the need for fighter-versus-fighter combat was still very much alive, other nations have had a chance to put modern fighter tactics to the test. Among them, Israel has probably had the most experience, but the air forces of both India and Pakistan are among a sizeable number to have had occasion to test their theories on the subject.

There has also been a tendency to 'over-sophisticate' the modern fighter, to the extent that its effectiveness as a weapon to knock down enemy fighters can come near to being compromised. Brig Gen Robin Olds, no stranger to a fighter cockpit from World War Two to Vietnam, summed up this situation when, commenting on the duplicity of warning equipment built into the F-4D, he said:

'We switched it all off—all of it. It got too complicated, even for a two-man crew. We would never have scored the kills we did if we'd had to take account of all the distracting and sometimes conflicting information coming at us from all that equipment. We needed eyes outside the cockpit to see the MiGs, decide on our attack profiles and go get them.'

That last statement would have been one with which the First World War scout pilot would have instantly agreed. There would, to him, have been no other way to fight. Pilots of that era had an inherent suspicion of gadgetry, especially if they thought it interfered with the basic task of the fighter. Even greater comforts in the form of enclosed cockpits and life-preserving items such as parachutes were not readily welcomed.

Perhaps, though, the similarities of combat are nothing at all to do with men who fly fighter aircraft as a profession, nor with the people who design them. That things are much as they were is surely more a comment on the state of international politics than on any technological state-of-the-art of military aeronautics. While many nations could tomorrow send up one fighter with the power to destroy an entire city—a power that has existed since the 1950s—few regimes, no matter how despotic, have seen the gains to be had from such an act as worthwhile.

Not that there is cause for complacency. Although the threat of nuclear war between the super powers has receded, it is the smaller, politically less mature powers which now indulge in the sabre rattling. Nearly all of these have fighter aircraft small enough to fly under defensive radar and take out a major target. You no longer need a bomber with a big fat radar signature to open a war. That, perhaps, is the major advance in fighter design in recent decades, for it has become an awesome weapon in its own right. Indeed, there are relatively few aircraft in this category which do not, sooner or later in their development, become 'mud movers'. It is then that the situation moves from the classic fighter-versus-fighter tussle to something far more deadly. But again, to stop the fighter bomber getting through a net of guns and SAMs, the most effective piece of hardware is—and always has been—a fighter.

CHAPTER 1

'Never been so frightened . . .'

Dawn, 27 July 1917. Estrée Blanche aerodrome, France, on the Allied Western Front. The first men to rise that morning realised all too quickly that they were probably in for another day of 'dud' weather. But rain and the inevitable poor visibility did at least mean that there would be more time to overhaul and service the aeroplanes. There was little activity over the front, and there was every likelihood that No. 56 Squadron, Royal Flying Corps, would remain at Estrée for the time being, owing to the relatively static state of the ground fighting. After a fortnight in 'Blighty' on home defence duty, No. 56 had been back in France barely two weeks.

All ranks, from the Commanding Officer down to the lowliest driver, had welcomed the break in England, but there had been little action for the unit. On the return to France it was obvious that the unseasonal weather had not noticeably improved since the unit's absence. The summer days of 1917 were to remain generally dismal.

Commanding No. 56 at that time was Maj R. E. Blomfield, described in contemporary reports as a 'dapper little ringmaster'. Not one to let his men grow idle during periods of inaction, Blomfield had instigated early morning runs around the aerodrome and found work for the pilots alongside the ground crews in the hangars. But he was no martinet. Pilots enjoyed frequent breaks from duty when operational considerations permitted, a fact that undoubtedly helped forge the squadron's enviable reputation.

Desk-bound himself, and obliged to get around wth the aid of a stick, the popular major believed passionately in the job his command had been sent to France to do. He was determined to make No. 56 the equal of any squadron in the RFC, and preferably better. In Blomfield's view, the squadron existed only to shoot down the enemy. Nothing else mattered.

Notwithstanding this positive approach to the job in hand, Blomfield was not a man to overlook the finer things of life. Music was a particular passion for him, and with some boldness, at times verging on sheer 'neck', he instigated his own system of recruiting ground crews who were also accomplished musicians. Blomfield even went so far as to 'advertise' No. 56 as a squadron where such skills would be welcome. He approached those members of leading orchestras who were about to be called to the colours and 'swapped' them for men already in the service whose musical knowledge was scant or non-existent. In that way Blomfield created (and kept) one of the best squadron orchestras in the RFC.

He knew well enough that such an interest reduced boredom during periods of stand-down and, in general, increased individual efficiency at work and play and thereby improved the effectiveness of the squadron.

As the first unit to be equipped with the Royal Aircraft Factory S.E.5, No. 56 had been taking delivery of new aircraft since April. The new fighter had not come on the scene a moment too soon. The RFC's humiliating performance against the German *Jagdstaffeln* during 'Bloody April' was all too fresh in the memory, but now the S.E. and Sopwith Camel offered the potential to meet the enemy on better than equal terms.

Both new British fighters were tangible evidence that, at last, the capability of the aeroplane in war had been recognised. Early in July 1917 the opening session of a government cabinet committee had convened to consider the current state of Britain's air organisation and defence, particularly in regard to German air attacks on southern England. The findings were not particularly encouraging, and it was seen that the front-line squadrons badly needed to be re-equipped with modern machines.

Little if any news of these deliberations in Westminster filtered through to fighter pilots on the Western Front—it is doubtful whether they would, in their own words, have 'cared a jot' about them. The jawing of politicians would have been taken with a healthy pinch of salt, for what these men needed was something better with which to fight. They, and they alone, it seemed, knew the high calibre of the enemy. If any further evidence were needed one had only to scrutinise the casualty figures for the spring of 1917.

The squadron was fortunate in having a nucleus of skilled, battle-hardened

The third prototype S.E.5, A4563, with a modified coaming behind the pilot's cockpit and a four-bladed propeller for the 200 h.p. Hispano-Suiza engine. This machine was issued to No. 56 Squadron on 11 June 1917. (Stuart Leslie)

pilots. It was through their efforts that the unit's reputation for prowess in the air was growing, but it had not been won without cost. May had been a particularly bad month. Barely was it a week old when the redoubtable Albert Ball, then commanding No. 56's 'A' Flight, had been lost in action.

On that same day, 7 May, Lt Roger Chaworth-Musters had gone down, and Henry 'Duke' Meintjes was wounded. Another loss to the squadron was Lt T. M. Dickinson, who became a prisoner of war on 4 June.

Gradually, the nature of the air war over the Western Front was changing. Increasing numbers of German fighters virtually spelled the end of the 'lone wolf' individualists of the past. Safety in numbers was now the RFC's watchword, heralding a significant rethinking of aerial tactics and pointing the way to the mutually protective formations that, for fighters, was to remain fundamentally unchanged.

Air combats were lasting longer as the duration of improved fighter aircraft was extended, and it was not unusual at that period of the war for over 50 aircraft to duel with each other for up to an hour. Typically, the escort to the vital reconnaissance machines operated over the front by both sides would become involved with the enemy scout squadrons, whose pilots did their best to shoot down the lightly-defended observation aircraft and deny the enemy up-to-date information of the situation on the ground.

This had always been, and was to remain, one of the primary reasons for putting aeroplanes and balloons into the air over the front. What later came to be called 'air superiority' over a given sector of the front enabled either side to carry out observation flights unhindered by enemy scouts. But the situation was rarely static for long. The RFC pilots noted intense enemy activity in the air, then periods when the enemy would not been seen in large numbers. Also by 1917, operations by bomb-carrying fighters became an increasingly important factor. Ground strafing had also entered the picture, and if such operations could be co-ordinated with infantry advances, some ground could be gained. Initially, the psychological effect on troops of being attacked by aeroplanes was tremendous—equal if not greater than the appearance of the first tanks on the battlefield.

Both sides grasped the potential of the aeroplane as a ground-attack weapon, although the RFC tended to regard it as a supplement to the business of aerial combat. The Germans, on the other hand, raised specialist units to undertake these demanding operations and to make operational tests of techniques and weapons that might make such attacks more effective.

While the Germans began at this time to operate in large numbers which the RFC pilots dubbed 'circuses', owing to a proliferation of exotic, gaudy colour schemes on the enemy machines, the basic British tactical unit was a flight of five or six aircraft, echeloned up. The flight leader led from the lowest position in the formation, and all other pilots simply had to look down, rather than up into the glare of the sun, to see his hand signals or the manoeuvres made by his aircraft. Thus an RFC scout formation resembled a huge 'V' in the sky from ahead or behind, as well as from above or below.

It was found that six was the maximum number of scouts one man could effectively control in the air, although three flights could be co-ordinated by the leader. Three-flight formations were found to be sufficient to take on the large enemy formations but, however high the total number of dogfighting aeroplanes, combat came down quickly to flights and single machines.

Each flight—usually identified by the initial letter 'A', 'B' or 'C'—was under the command of an experienced pilot. All flights invariably adopted the standard Vee formation, with the squadron CO leading the lowest element and with the other two echeloned out two to three hundred yards on either side. That gave the RFC an effective tactical strength of fifteen to eighteen machines on offensive patrols.

The solitary foray over enemy lines was not entirely a thing of the past, however; numerous British pilots chanced the solo sortie which could catch the Germans napping. Success still came against ground targets and the less-vigilant enemy pilot when the element of surprise was achieved. One pilot of No. 56 Squadron who continued to fly the occasional lone sortie was Geoffrey Hilton Bowman.

A newcomer to No. 56, but not to air fighting, Bowman had been posted to the squadron on 11 May 1917, when it was stationed at Vert Galant in northern France. He was one of the replacements for the casualties of 7 May, which actually totalled four—two killed and two wounded.

Bowman took command of 'C' Flight, remaining for a time an acting flight commander. Both he and Albert Ball's replacement at the head of 'A' Flight, Capt Phillip Prothero, were a little 'rusty' on the latest tactics, and consequently all three flights were led for a short period by the remaining flight commander, Capt C. M. 'Billy' Crowe.

Bowman did not take long to bring himself up to date. On 27 May he shot down a two-seater and beat a hasty retreat over the lines with five German scouts in pursuit. This was his third victory, the first two having been scored while he was a member of No. 29 Squadron. Like the other pilots of No. 56, Bowman was beginning to appreciate the worth of the S.E.5. Men like Arthur Rhys Davids, Leonard Barlow, Richard Maybery and Eric Turnbull were among those who, with a fine fighter in their hands, were prepared for whatever the enemy might put against them.

While the S.E.5 brought forth much admiration for its performance, it had numerous teething troubles. Developed under the impetus of war, it had not been thoroughly tested before being issued to front-line units, and No. 56 was responsible for operational testing of numerous modifications that 'improved the breed'.

In the early days of the S.E.5's service, few men worked harder than the engine fitters. Production standards governing the volume manufacture of engines varied considerably, and each aircraft off the production lines had its own idiosyncracies. Force of circumstance obliged the Royal Aircraft Factory to accept engines from a number of manufacturers, and some of these were decidedly below even basic standards of reliability. A knock-on effect was that the spares supply situation was also bad. Replacement engines were in very short supply during the summer of 1917 and, even when spares did arrive at the front, there was no guarantee that they would fit existing squadron aircraft without a degree of modification.

With regular, skilled maintenance the S.E.'s Hispano-Suiza engine would last about 20 hours between major overhauls—on average that would equate to one

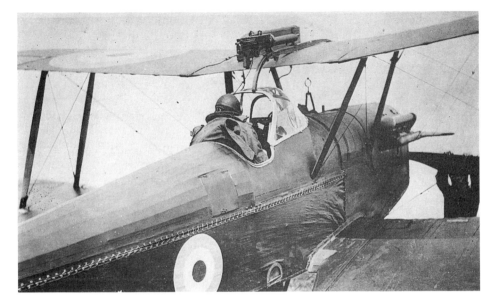

Lt S. Broadberry prepares to fly A8903, an S.E.5 of the second production batch with a gravity-feed fuel tank mounted alongside the Lewis gun, an arrangement dispensed with on the S.E.5a. A mechanic awaits the pilot's signal to swing the prop. (S. Leslie)

aircraft flying 15 patrols. While that figure was not good, the general situation in 1917 was far worse. It was found, for example, that Wolseley-built crankshafts were typically good for only four hours at operational revolutions. Equally

An overall view of the aircraft in the previous photograph, taken at the same time, with the same pilot. The 'Lift Here' instruction on the rear fuselage has been applied in elegant white script. (S. Leslie)

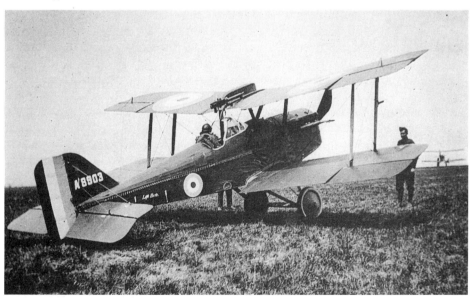

Above left *Although it offered a greater degree of protection from the slipstream, the 'wrap-around' windscreen of the early production S.E.5s was not welcomed by RFC pilots, who feared it would shatter in a bad landing accident. There was the additional hazard from Perspex shards if the screen was hit by enemy fire during combat. An abbreviated windscreen was fitted by No. 56 Squadron in the field. This view also shows the Lewis gun pulled fully down the Foster mount for rearming. (S. Leslie via Garry Nelson)*

Above right *A good study of the S.E.5a's armament, showing the unique Foster 'slide' mounting for the top-plane Lewis .303 in machine-gun. The single Vickers on the port side of the forward upper cowling has its own ring sight, and the twin mounting rings for an Aldis sight are directly in front of the windscreen. Also clearly seen is the proximity of the exhaust pipe to the cockpit. Geoffrey Bowman was probably not alone among S.E. pilots in momentarily forgetting how near (and how hot) this pipe was, and suffering resultant burns when getting out in a hurry. (S. Leslie via G. Nelson)*

taxing for ground crews were frequent cases of distortion of the thin exhaust valves, which led to overheating of the cylinders and a chain reaction of problems that, if undetected, would cause an engine to seize in a very short time. The root cause of the hot cylinders was uneven heat treatment of helical pinions during manufacture.

There were other drawbacks to the S.E. in its 'as delivered' condition. Among these was the infernal 'greenhouse' windscreen, which quickly became an object of derision. The factory had fitted the screen with the best intention of protecting the pilot from the icy slipstream blast at altitude. While that was laudable, the pilots, long used to the rigours of flying aircraft with open cockpits, had other concerns. They feared that a man's face would be cut to ribbons by Perspex shards from a screen shattered in a crash, or through enemy action.

The squadron waited until all of its S.E.s were safely back in France, away from the critical gaze of higher authority, before ordering the removal of the windscreens from all aircraft. They were replaced by small windshields which did

Dominated by the breech of the fuselage-mounted Vickers machine-gun, the cockpit of this S.E.5a shows the basic instrumentation of a First World War scout. The large petrol cock is in the centre of the panel, with the compass and airspeed indicator on the right. The top of the control column is also visible. (S. Leslie via G. Nelson)

not wrap around the sides of the cockpit. It took about a week to carry out the job.

On the plus side, the S.E.5 was a strong aircraft, well able to withstand the stresses imposed by aerial maneouvres in combat. Pilots appreciated the excellent view from the cockpit, which was comfortable and, by First World War standards, quite warm. The fact that the aircraft was easy to fly endeared it to those with less experience on scouts, and when everything functioned smoothly it had adequate power in hand to allow speed to build up for a vertical zoom

The cockpits of individual S.E.5as from different production batches displayed numerous detail differences. Although it is not apparent in this view, the Vickers .303 in machine-gun is in position on this aircraft, which has a rounded lower edge to the windscreen and lacks any padding on the cockpit rim. (S. Leslie via G. Nelson)

climb, a favourite RFC tactic in 1917.

It was found, however, that in such a climb the pilot had to use his guns quickly, as the S.E. would lose speed as the angle increased and eventually stall out. While the RFC's principal fighter adversaries enjoyed a greater service ceiling than either the S.E.5 or the Camel (17,000 and 19,000 ft respectively), the British aircraft had better endurance and both were faster than the Albatros D.V and Fokker Dr.1, both of which could reach an altitude of 20,000 ft.

Enemy height advantage—'the Hun in the sun'—could still give the British squadrons a serious challenge, although, as with virtually every air battle ever fought, a great deal depended on the circumstances in which each side came upon the other, the number of aircraft involved and, above all, the skill of individual pilots.

Success or failure could hinge very much on the manner in which combat was joined. If one side had a height advantage, the crucial element of surprise could be exploited. If surprise was maintained, the sudden, classic 'stab in the back' could exact a substantial toll from the enemy formation, enough for it break up and beat a hasty retreat, not through fear but for fundamental self-preservation. The adage: 'he who fights and runs away, may live to fight another day' was sound. Both sides suffered losses when pilots failed to see an enemy scout sliding in behind them, let alone hear it above the roar of their own engine.

By the early summer of 1917 No. 56 Squadron had a complement of about 30 pilots and an establishment of 32 S.E.5s. In company with Nos 19 (Spad VII) and 66 (Sopwith Pup) Squadrons, it formed part of the 9th Wing of the RFC. WIth approximately 100 scouts on hand, the Wing allocated patrol areas to each unit, No. 56 having responsibility for a sector of the front out to Houthulst Forest, Roulers, Menin and Quesnoy.

Air actions directly in support of the third battle of Ypres—the notorious 'Wipers' in infantryman's parlance—had started for the RFC on 11 June, with a series of bombing raids on enemy aerodromes and rail junctions on the 2nd and 5th Army fronts. The tempo gradually quickened, and spirited German reaction to British patrols resulted in some of the largest dogfights yet seen over the Western Front.

At the start of July, Geoffrey Bowman (who, incidentally, had picked up the nickname 'Beery' during the course of his service career, apparently with regard to his ruddy complexion rather than his drinking habits) had seven victories to his credit. These comprised six aeroplanes and one observation balloon.

It was reckoned that *Vizefeldwebel* Fritz Krebs of Jasta 6 closely matched Bowman in terms of flying skill, but his promising career as a fighter pilot was abruptly terminated when the two men crossed swords. On 16 July Krebs met his match when Bowman shot his Albatros down in flames over Polygon Wood.

No. 56 claimed three victories that day, during a period of heavy air fighting. Five more German aircraft were to fall to the guns of the squadron on the 20th, one going to Bowman. Despite this success, Beery was apparently dissatisfied with his personal scoring rate, and two days later set out on another solo patrol which was something of an experiment.

Bowman found his quarry, an enemy scout, over Cambrai, and tried to despatch it by dropping a pineapple bomb on it. Whether or not Bowman's guns had jammed is not recorded, but the result was a failure, the missile failing to find its target. Air fighting above the trenches grew more intense as the Allied armies continued to plan the assault that would eventually secure the Ypres salient. The horror of the third Ypres battle was compounded by the weather. Higher-than-average rainfall for the time of year turned the battlefield into a sea of mud, and, churned up by countless shells, the area became a graveyard of horrendous proportions. Had they ever been forced to choose, pilots of the RFC would surely have opted to face three times the number of enemy scouts in every dogfight rather than endure the suffering of their comrades in arms on the ground.

The squadron was regularly putting up multiple patrols during the course of a single day, and on 26 July the S.E.s clashed with the enemy once again. German fire accounted for yet another of the squadron's flight commanders when Phillip Prothero, still leading 'A' Flight, was shot down. The day brought more adverse weather, keeping air action to a minimum, but by evening the skies had cleared sufficiently for No. 56 to meet the Germans over Polygon Wood.

The S.E.s encountered formations of Albatros scouts acting as top cover for reconnaissance two-seaters, and a sizeable dogfight ensued. In the melée, which involved a total of 94 aircraft, Capt Prothero's S.E. was badly hit. It was last seen falling with both starboard wings broken off.

July was the month that 56 Squadron received examples of the S.E.5a. The final production S.E.5s were regarded as the first of the 5a models, as they featured the latter's reduced wingspan. The performance of the S.E.5a was improved over that of the earlier version; it was some ten miles an hour faster and could reach a ceiling of 17,000 ft, 500 ft more than an S.E.5 in typical front-line condition. As indicated earlier, however, the performance of individual aircraft varied, sometimes quite considerably. The improved S.E. was welcomed by 56 Squadron. Although its performance did not quite match that of the Camel, which had few equals in terms of manoeuvrability, many of the top RFC pilots swore by it.

An interesting line-up of No. 56 Squadron machines soon after receipt of the S.E.5a. Most of the aircraft have the original factory-fitted wrap-around windscreen. Identifiable serial numbers are A4863, A4855 and A4854. Albert Ball's A4850 is in the centre of the photo, behind A4850. (S. Leslie)

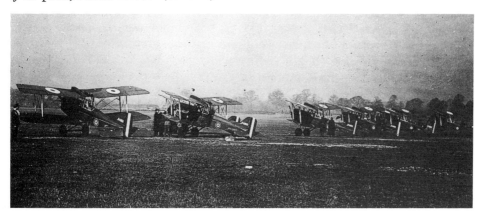

Geoffrey Bowman was issued with one of the first S.E.5as, and he is believed to have flown it until September, when it was badly damaged in a forced landing. Replacement of the earlier type by the S.E.5a was carried out as fast as deliveries would allow, and for some time the squadron operated with a mix of both.

On 27 July the skies again cleared as evening approached. Late afternoon patrols were popular with pilots, as the low angle of the setting sun tended to nullify any natural advantage to either side. The air was also less turbulent for the light scouts, and if aircraft suffered combat damage it was relatively easy for a pilot to make a prudent exit from the battle area using the rapidly fading light as cover.

That day No. 56 became embroiled in a wild fight, the squadron pitting its S.E.s against a strong formation of Albatros D.Vs, the famed 'V-Strutters'. Geoffrey Bowman's experience was, to say the least, 'hairy'.

The British aircraft had reached their patrol area east of the Roulers-Menin road when a formation of nine enemy aircraft was spotted. As combat was joined, two of them singled out Bowman's machine for attack.

Forced to drop from 14,000 to 4,000 ft, Bowman also had one gun out of action. In a situation that was becoming increasingly 'shaky', he needed all his flying skill to evade the enemy fire. Then, as so often happens in air combat, the situation changed. Lt Maybery had seen Bowman's predicament and waded in, shooting one Albatros off Beery's tail. The other German scout fled.

Turning east, Bowman was immediately attacked by another German scout, a machine he later described as being painted red all over. It was also, he noted, 'very well flown'. Still with only one gun working, Bowman descended to around 1,000 ft, his adversary following and repeating a set technique of attack—a dive to open fire, then a zoom away into a climbing turn to come in again on the S.E.'s tail.

Finally, seeing his quarry flying towards the British lines, the German changed tactics. After yet another attack he broke off, made a zoom climb, then stall turned to come in again, this time from head-on. It was a fatal manoeuvre. Bowman carefully judged his opponent's dive, snapped his throttle back and watched the red Albatros overshoot. Now he had his chance.

Climbing to get above the enemy machine, Bowman took sight and fired the Lewis gun on the top wing. Fifty rounds at 20 ft range more than did the trick. The aggressive German fell away to dive vertically into the ground. Watching it crash, Bowman reflected that the enemy pilot had given him but one chance to fire during the entire engagement. Had he not grown impatient and changed his mode of attack, Bowman might not have had that chance.

At that point Bowman's Lewis decided to pack up—just as another Albatros latched on to him. Jinking and diving even lower, the defenceless S.E. must have seemed easy meat. But Bowman had managed to persuade his fuselage-mounted Vickers gun to work again, and he turned into the Albatros and fired. There was no immediate effect, but the German was too low. Preoccupied with trying to keep out of the S.E.'s field of fire, he failed to see the danger looming. His aircraft crashed straight into a tree on the edge of Houthulst Forest.

Flying down-sun, Bowman skirted the forest. It was well past time to be getting home. Then three more German scouts appeared, probably thinking

S.E.5a C5303/X, with Lt Franklin in the cockpit. (S. Leslie)

they had found themselves an easy victim. Although the same thought might have crossed Bowman's mind, he was determined to show them otherwise. He prudently made for the British lines, zooming and diving to present the worst possible target for the Spandau rounds coming his way. Finally the S.E. crossed the lines at the Ysar Canal, by Het Sas. Bowman skimmed over the British

A modified S.E.5a, A8911/A-3, in a hangar at Estrée Blanche, France, showing the individual aircraft identification repeated on the fuselage spine. This machine was flown regularly by Eric Turnbull, a contemporary of Geoffrey Bowman during his time on No. 56 Squadron. (S. Leslie)

trenches at 50 ft and landed safely at Estrée Blanche. He later committed his emotions to the pages of his log book, ending with the heartfelt words: 'Never been so frightened in my life'.

Geoffrey Bowman's combat of 27 July contained many elements typical of a Western Front dogfight from the British viewpoint at that time, including the superior number of enemy scouts, the all-too-common malfunction of armament, and the undeniable calibre of individual enemy pilots and their machines. A not inconsiderable factor was the 'neutral' part played by natural hazards when fighting took place at very low altitude. Too many fine pilots ended their careers by flying their flimsy machines into trees and other obstacles while being distracted by what was going on behind them. Sometimes such crashes were survivable, and numerous pilots ended a flight with their aircraft perched high in the branches of tall trees, a somewhat embarrassing position. It was when the aircraft flew very low and hit the trunks of trees that fatalities occurred.

The combat survived by Bowman contained other elements that could be, and were, adapted and revised to give the RFC a winning edge over the German *Jagdstaffeln* by the time the war ended, although it is true to say that both sides were often evenly matched. Each side had to learn to be adaptable in combat, and not to dismiss a good idea even if it did originate with the enemy. The Germans were perhaps quicker to appreciate the value of a second pair of eyes when a dogfight broke formations into smaller elements. The evolution of the wingman system was slow, but there was no question that it was sound.

The passing of the 'chivalrous' phase of the air war was not universally accepted by either side; air fighting had started out as something akin to a deadly game of chance, but it soon turned into a ruthless 'kill or be killed' contest with little thought spared for the fate of the pilot on the wrong end of a stream of machine-gun fire. That is not to say that the human element was entirely forgotten, as the fate of a vanquished pilot could often be observed from an open cockpit during the relatively slow pace of combat. Most pilots who had been in action for any length of time realised all too well what the war had become, and many confided their fears and abhorrence in diaries and note-books. Inevitably there were a few who could not adapt.

August was a momentus month for 56 Squadron. James McCudden was posted to the unit as a flight commander with his score standing at 11, one less than Bowman. McCudden had already had a taste of life on No. 56 when he had taken an S.E.5a out on patrol with the unit on 21 July. Major Blomfield obviously thought that the young pilot from Kent would be an invaluable asset, and McCudden duly arrived on 14 August. His meteoric scoring rate showed Blomfield's judgement to be as sound as ever.

Bowman, meanwhile, continued to add to his own 'bag' of enemy aircraft, weathering periods when contact with the *Jagdstaffeln* brought inconclusive results to both sides. Flying over the Western Front in 1917 was, however, rarely without its moments of excitement.

On 15 August Bowman was on an evening patrol with 'C' Flight. Take-off time was 18:15, and Bowman led the patrol, flying S.E.5a B8906. Little evidence of German activity could be found in the air, but the increasing danger from ground-strafing aeroplanes made gunners on the ground jumpy. To certain batteries, aeroplanes—any aeroplanes—spelt danger. The crews were not always briefed as to whose aircraft might be approaching their position at a given time, and quite often opened up without warning. Bowman's patrol had been out for about $1\frac{3}{4}$ hrs when 'Archie' let rip, hitting his machine in the radiator.

Severely damaged, the overheating S.E. refused to fly much further and there was nothing for it but to put down as quickly as possible. Bowman just managed to reach the British front line, the wheels of his machine coming to rest a bare 2,000 yd inside friendly territory near Lens.

After claiming an Albatros during an evening patrol on 22 August (the enemy scout apparently went down out of control), Bowman went on leave for two weeks. It was early September before he returned to 56 Squadron.

On the 6 September Bowman suffered an unfortunate accident. He had just landed, and McCudden went over to the S.E. as it taxied in to discuss something. It was more than likely the news that the morning patrol had come across two new German scouts, the Fokker Dr.1 triplane and the Pfalz D.III. Bowman, listening to his colleague, swung a leg over the edge of the cockpit to climb out, and forgot about the hot exhaust pipe. The fact that he was wearing shorts made the situation worse, and McCudden later wrote that the smell of roast pork was most appetizing! Bowman was obliged to spend the next few weeks with his leg bandaged.

September 1917 was to be long remembered in the annals of the RFC, for on the 23rd the evening patrol put up by 56 Squadron met the German ace Leutnant Werner Voss, *Kommandeur* of Jasta 10. The day of the autumn equinox was fading fast as Voss latched on to the tail of a solitary S.E.5a and promptly harried it over the darkening fields of Flanders. The pursuit was

2nd Lt Barclay McPherson in what was probably his personal aircraft for a time. The long 'perforated' exhaust pipe fitted to late production S.E.5as is visible. McPherson became a PoW on 1 April 1918. (S. Leslie)

observed by members of 56 Squadron, then heading in from the east. Bowman was among them.

The British formation was led by McCudden, with Rhys Davids, Maybery, Cronyn, Hoidge and Muspratt in close company. Against such redoubtable foes, it seemed as though even a pilot as good as Voss stood little chance, but a very tough fight was to follow, even though Voss was set up for the perfect trap. McCudden cleverly positioned his aircraft so that the German ace was caught in an open-ended box which had Rhys Davids on the opposite side to himself and with Muspratt and Hoidge above and below. The other two British fighters in the flight were positioned to block any possible escape route. More Allied scouts had arrived on the scene, as had German reinforcements, although the latter were largely kept away from the S.E. versus triplane combat.

Three times the British pilots attempted to drive Voss down, and three times he turned on them like a cornered tiger. Bullets sprayed in every direction as the German ace fought for his life. A number of S.E.s were holed. Bowman and R. Stuart-Wortley were among those who observed the amazing antics of the triplane as it strove to break the trap.

A brave Albatros D.V pilot intervened to cover Voss, but was driven down. The predicament in which Voss found himself did not, Bowman later reported, 'appear to deter him in the slightest'.

It was felt that the unequal contest could have been broken off at almost any point by Voss, who appeared to have plenty of ammunition. There was enough cover in the gathering twilight for him to have made good his escape, but instead he chose to fight it out, constantly turning in to his attackers and performing some of the most amazing aerobatics the British pilots had yet

Lt Harold 'Jackie' Walkerdine and his groundcrew pose with B8266, an S.E.5a of No. 56 Squadron which was coded 'Y'. (S. Leslie)

witnessed. Despite their fire, the triplane seemed almost indestructible.

At last Rhys Davids got in a telling burst which raked the Fokker from end to end and, apparently, wounded Voss. Erratic flight, such as that which the triplane was now displaying, was a sure sign of an incapacitated pilot, but Rhys Davids made sure with more bursts from both the Vickers and Lewis guns. Finally the German scout fell slowly to earth, where observers saw it disintegrate into dust.

It was not until the following day that 56 Squadron was informed of the identity of the fallen German pilot. That he had been among the best of air fighters was in little doubt—the number of patches required on the S.E.s involved in the combat testified to that. Rhys Davids and McCudden were in agreement that, had it been possible, they would have preferred him to have come down alive. They were not alone in believing that Werner Voss was the greatest German pilot they had met in combat, more skilled even than the vaunted Manfred von Richthofen.

Bowman's personal score continued to climb steadily. He added another Albatros on 28 September; and the following day the squadron could proudly announce that its total of enemy aircraft destroyed had reached 200. This was more than adequate compensation for all the good work the squadron had done, but, in war, any collective feeling of confidence can be quickly overshadowed by events, as No. 56 was to find out in October.

During the evening patrol on the 1st, Lt R. H. Sloley was lost in a dogfight with Pfalz and Albatros scouts. Mixing it with a group of German pilots who knew their job, the S.E. pilots had a hard time keeping them at bay. Nevertheless, one Albatros was shot down and B Flight shared a second.

The dogfight in which the 2 October evening patrol became involved was inconclusive, due to both B and C Flights being badly positioned. Although both sides used their guns, nobody scored, and a disgusted Bowman, noting that the RFC had failed to dominate the battle, confided to his diary 'driven out of the sky twice'. About the only interesting observation on the 2 October patrol was that the Germans were reliably reported to be flying Fokker Dr.1 triplanes, when it was understood that supplies of this new type had not then been received by operational *Jastas* in any numbers.

There followed a period of stand-down under a cloak of bad weather, and although he flew a number of patrols during October, Bowman experienced another of his 'quiet' periods. It was not until near the end of October that he was again involved in a large-scale air battle.

Having achieved some success during the late summer months, the Allied ground armies were forced to pause as appalling weather conditions made any forward movement a nightmare. Just as a breakthrough seemed imminent, troops, guns, men and equipment became bogged down in a sea of mud. A success in Flanders still lay in the future. There seemed to be little prospect of an end to the continual back-and-forth fighting.

On 27 October 56 Squadron put up seven S.E.s for the morning patrol at 10:40, with Bowman leading Jarvis, Muspratt, Slingsby, Coote, Maybery and Rhys Davids. A mile southwest of Roulers Bowman spotted two enemy scout formations. A thousand feet below were two Pfalz D. IIIs—-probably acting as bait for unwary Allied pilots who spotted them and failed to look up, where six

Albatros D.Vs prowled. Bowman was too experienced to fall for such a ruse, and indicated that the others should attack the German high cover while he dived on the two Pfalz.

Getting into a good position, Beery fired about 40 rounds from both guns and one Pfalz went down, in what Bowman described as 'a quick spiral'. Keeping a wary eye on the other Pfalz, he dived after his victim, but at 1,000 ft he broke off the chase, having failed to get the enemy machine in his sights for another telling burst. He climbed to rejoin his flight.

The intermittent running dual with the German scouts lasted almost two hours. Bowman re-formed the flight, but by the time he did so, the action had petered out. Three S.E.5s were missing.

Back at Estrée Blanche the squadron was pleased to hear that two pilots, Maybery and Slingsby, had made safe forced landings, but nobody had seen Rhys Davids go down. The optimistic speculation that this popular pilot had survived to become a prisoner persisted for some time, but hopes faded as no official word was received. No word of his fate ever did come to light, and he was still posted as missing in action at the end of the war. Decades passed before evidence was unearthed to suggest that Arthur Rhys Davids' last flight ended when Leutnant Karl Gallwitz, acting *Staffelfuhrer* of *Jasta Boelke*, shot him down.

Another three weeks passed, during which the Allies launched yet another attempt to break the Western Front deadlock, before Bowman claimed his 19th victory, on 23 November. All of the squadron's aircraft were up, from a new

Lt Fielding-Johnson in S.E.5a B37, with the rear fairing behind the cockpit removed, a not uncommon 'modification' on 56 Squadron's aircraft. The relatively plain markings shown were used by No. 56 until the end of the war, although the distinctive white band was dropped in March 1918. Lack of colourful markings did not preclude dash and daring in the air, but the RFC's German adversaries were garish in comparison with the generally sober finish of British scouts. (S. Leslie)

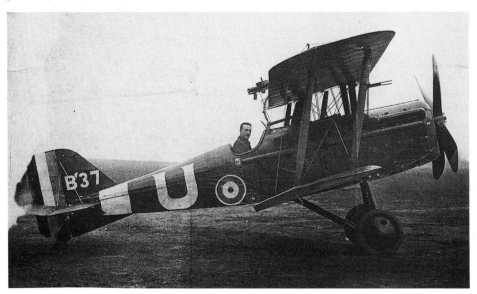

base at Lavieville, and single victories were also scored by McCudden and Harmon. A further two weeks then passed before Bowman's log book could again record significant action. As many pilots found throughout this and other aerial conflicts, 'action' was not always of the kind desired.

On 10 December Bowman was heading north, leading a formation of S.E.5s, when he spotted a German observation balloon over the Bois de Vaucelles. The enemy had launched another counter-attack some two weeks before, and had forced the Allied front line back. It was becoming a grimly familiar pattern.

Leading his aircraft down to strafe the lame target, Bowman checked behind him when he was still about one hundred feet above it—and found that a formation of German scouts was also diving. There was little doubt of their target.

Pulling up very hard, the British pilot realised that he had over-stressed his S.E., and three of its wingtips promptly collapsed. The aircraft dropped some distance out of control, and seeing the wings 'wobbling like jelly', Bowman carefully turned and headed for the British lines, flying as steadily as possible so as not to impose any further strain. By keeping his airspeed below 65 m.p.h., Beery made it. After he had landed he vowed never to go near a balloon again. When his S.E. was examined it was found to have broken spars outboard of the struts on all three of the damaged wings.

On 19 December No. 56 suffered another grievous loss when Richard Maybery failed to return from a patrol. It was some weeks before it was learned he had been killed after fellow pilots had seen his machine falling, out of control.

Bowman went on leave over the Christmas period of 1917, and on 9 January 1918 56 Squadron was able to celebrate 250 victories. This milestone also included the 100th kill for McCudden's own Flight, the British ace having despatched the aircraft in question, an LVG two-seater. That month the unit made another change of base, to Baizieux.

Bowman's more modest personal score grew when he returned to the fray later in January. On the 28th he made it 20 by shooting down a Pfalz D. III in flames. Then Bowman was promoted from Captain to Major that same month, and offered a posting to command No. 41 Squadron. Although he was not at all keen to leave No. 56, the command of a squadron was not an opportunity to be missed. Bowman prepared to leave, but only with the proviso that he be allowed to take his beloved S.E.5a with him.

Other changes in 56 Squadron were afoot; McCudden was also to bid farewell to the unit a few weeks after Bowman. Tragically, the young man from Kent who had destroyed 57 enemy aircraft was to die in April from injuries received in a non-operational accident, having just taken up a posting at the head of 60 Squadron.

Bowman replaced the CO of No. 41 Squadron at Lealvilliers on 9 February, after Maj F. J. Powell had been shot down and become a PoW. The squadron had re-equipped with the S.E.5a in November 1917, having previously flown the F.E.8 and D.H.5, primarily in the ground-attack role. Its S.E.s were also heavily engaged on this type of work, and the unit was very busy during the early period of the German spring offensive.

This massive assault, aimed at finally breaking the Western Front deadlock, had started with an artillery bombardment on 21 March. Five days later the

French and British established a unified command to ensure that the advancing Germans could be contained by feeding troops into sectors as they were threatened. By the 28th, despite heavy Allied casualties, there were signs that the enemy had reached the limit of his 40-mile penetration into the Allied lines. For the Germans, Operation Michael had failed. It was to seal the fate of the nation.

Administrative tasks which are the lot of a squadron commander kept Geoffrey Bowman on the ground more than he would have liked, but he did fly patrols when the 'sea of bumph' subsided a little. On 16 February he succeeded in driving down a two-seater over Bantouzelle, and followed this with another German reconnaissance machine, found patrolling over Berjanmont later that day. These victories brought his score to 22.

Late in May, Bowman had another unfortunate accident which could, this time, have proved fatal. Diving on a Rumpler over Don, the drum of his Lewis gun came off and struck his head with such force that he was rendered unconscious. Bowman reckoned that the S.E.5a fell 5,000 ft before he came round and brought the aircraft under control.

As the spring of 1918 turned to summer, it was fairly obvious that the Germans were at their last gasp. With the spring offensive stalled, the Allies prepared for their own decisive attack. It came on 8 August. Spearheaded by the usual artillery bombardment and the 'new fangled' tanks, plus a significant number of Australian and Canadian troops, the British and French armies pressed forward. This time the advance would not be stopped.

In common with other scout squadrons, No. 40 was in the thick of the fighting to support the men on the ground, flying numerous ground strafing

A manufacturer's study of S.E.5a C6481 after completion at the Royal Aircraft Factory. (Bruce Robertson)

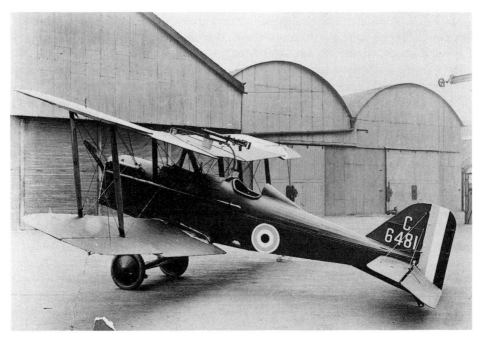

sorties to harry and demoralise the retreating enemy. After another spell of leave, Bowman returned to the Western Front in July, and on the 17th he brought down a Rumpler which lost its port elevator to his fire. The German was last seen in a flat spin over Bapaume.

On the day after the start of the Allied 'big push', Bowman was on patrol when he tangled with a Fokker D.VII, one of the finest fighters produced by the Germans during the conflict. On this occasion however, good equipment availed the enemy pilot little, for it was he who went down.

While the new Royal Air Force, created on 1 April 1918, was much less like a generously sized friendly flying club than the Royal Flying Corps had been in the early days, the fighting area of the Western Front was still small enough for individuals to visit their comrades in the 'old squadron' without being away too long. Bowman dropped in on No. 56 whenever he had the chance, to renew old acquaintances. Among the new faces, he found some of the old stagers, including Blomfield, who had in Bowman's absence been promoted to the rank of colonel. Blomfield was to relinquish the command of 56 Squadron to Maj R. D. Balcombe-Brown in November, and the unit was to have yet another CO before the end of the war, when Maj E. L. S. H. Gilchrist took over in May 1918.

Numbers 56 and 41 squadrons were to remain part of the 13th (Army) Wing until August 1918, when the latter became part of the 22nd Wing. Earlier re-jigging of RFC Wing strengths had seen the transfer of No. 56 from the 9th Wing during the autumn of 1917.

More victories were added to Beery's personal tally in September, including another Fokker D.VII north of Roulers on the 16th, a Fokker D.VII which was last seen going down out of control over Houthulst Forest and, on the 25th, a Rumpler which he shot down in flames. Two days later, Bowman was ordered to make sure he stayed on the friendly side of the lines.

In total, Bowman scored eight more kills with 41 Squadron, including a Fokker D.VII on 10 October. Flying with Capt F. O. 'Mongoose' Soden, he pounced on the enemy scout after it had shot down a British balloon. It fell into British held territory.

Soden subsequently forced down the Fokker D.VIII flown by Leutnant Hans Auer, on 28 October. As it had landed intact, Bowman was among those who took the chance to examine the German machine at close quarters, and was photographed nonchalantly perched on one of its main wheels.

Another victory, which turned out to be Bowman's last, came on the 15th of the month, when, on a day that recorded little other air activity over the Allied front line, he was alerted by British 'Archie' bursting west of Roulers. After diving 7,000 ft to locate what the gunners were aiming at, he found a formation of ten Fokkers. Bowman pumped 100 rounds into the aircraft flown by the leader. The weight of fire caused the enemy scout's top mainplane to buckle, whereupon the aircraft went down.

Bearing in mind the recent order for him not to risk being shot down behind enemy lines, Bowman was reluctant to report this victory, even though he saw the wreck of the enemy machine on the ground. He knew that the RAF could ill-afford to lose experienced flight commanders, even at that late stage of the war, and that it was foolhardy to tempt fate. Unfortunately, his victory was reported by Belgian troops—and another order came through.

This time the spirited British ace was left in no doubt that he was not only expressly forbidden to fly across the lines, but he was not to fly at all. But after less than a week kicking his heels on the ground, Bowman was back in the air.

So fast was the British advance of 1918 that even the airmen had difficulty keeping up with it. Bowman was out on 25 October and flying over friendly troops who had laid out a message in the form of a large white 'V' on the ground. Returning to base, Bowman found out that this was a request for air delivery of small-arms ammunition. Although he promptly loaded two sandbags with bullets, plus cigarettes, and flew back to the area, he could find no indication that the troops had waited.

With the British having penetrated the Hindenburg Line, the French and Americans following through with their offensive in the Argonne, and a British, Belgian and French army group making good progress in the Flanders region, it was clearly the beginning of the end for Germany. As early as 29 September Ludendorff concluded that all that was left was to start negotiations for a surrender.

Geoffrey Bowman's last patrol was flown on the morning of 11 November 1918. Within hours the armistice was signed, to end five years of bloodletting. There were then 16 squadrons equipped with the S.E.5a and 17 flying the Sopwith Camel on the Western Front. Number 56 Squadron ended up with 423 enemy aircraft destroyed for the loss of 39 pilots killed in action in 19 months of operations.

When the final RFC/RAF aerial victory lists were compiled, Bowman had been credited with 32 victories, making him the 20th top-scoring British Empire ace. He had been awarded the DFC, and a Military Cross was added on 17 September 1917. A bar was added to his MC on 27 October 1917, and he received the DSO in March 1918.

Bowman remained in command of 41 Squadron for a short period after the war, leaving the unit when it returned to the UK in February 1919. He stayed in the RAF and eventually rose to the rank of wing commander.

The present-day RAF rank titles were introduced officially on 17 August 1919, but that June Major Bowman had volunteered to join a British force in north Russia, operating on the side of White Russian forces against the new Bolshevik government. Never one to duck the chance of excitement, Bowman welcomed this break in peacetime routine. Upon arriving at Archangel he was given the command of the locally-raised 3 Squadron. There was also a 2 Squadron, but neither had any connection with similarly numbered units in the regular RAF.

Number 3 Squadron was equipped with the de Havilland D.H.9 and 9A, and the main task of the two squadrons was bombing and strafing attacks on Red forces ('Bolo' forces, as they were known to the British) occupying positions on the Dvina and Vaga rivers. There was little aerial opposition, but sorties were hazardous owing to considerable ground defences and the propensity of the Red forces to butcher anyone unfortunate enough to fall into their hands. Bowman himself undoubtedly flew a number of sorties during this sojourn, which was to be relatively brief. Inspired by Winston Churchill, it had little hope of turning the tide of the Russian revolution.

By the end of August rumours were rife that the RAF was destined to leave, and after a few more sorties in early September the work of the 'Relief Force' was terminated. It was widely felt that it had been little more than a waste of time, as the White Russian cause was clearly a lost one in the face of the strength of the Bolsheviks.

Bowman continued to visit numerous far-flung outposts of the Empire for some years. Fellow officers were amazed at Beery's habit of turning up in the most unlikely spots, where he would invariably be found in the mess, enthralling everyone with his experiences, telling jokes, and generally being the life and soul of the party.

Wg Cdr Bowman was a member of the headquarters staff, Inland Area in 1930. He died on 25 March 1970.

Pilots of No. 56 Squadron, Royal Flying Corps, 1917–18

Capt Albert Ball	KIA 7 May 17
Lt Leonard M. Barlow	
Lt Geoffrey H. Bowman	
Lt H. J. Burden	
Lt Roger Chaworth-Musters	KIA 7 May 17
Lt Maxwell H. Coote	
Capt V. P. Cronyn	
Capt Cyril M. 'Billy' Crowe	
Lt T. M. Dickinson	PoW 4 June 17
Lt Fielding-Johnson	
Capt E. L. Foot	
Lt Franklin	
Capt Duncan Grinnell-Milne	
Lt B. W. Harmon	
Capt Ian H. J. Henderson	
Lt R. T. C. Hoidge	
Capt L. W. Jarvis	
Lt M. A. Kay	KIA 30 April 17
Lt C. R. N. Knight	KIA 7 April 17
Lt K. J. Knaggs	
Lt J. O. Leech	
Lt H. M. T. Lehmann	
Capt Cecil A. Lewis	
Lt Gerald J. C. Maxwell	
Lt Richard A. Maybery	KIA 19 Dec 17
Lt M. E. Mealing	
Lt Henry 'Duke' Meintjes	KIA 7 May 17

Lt W. B. Melville   KIA 27 Oct 17
Lt Keith K. Muspratt
2nd Lt Eugene R. MacDonald
Maj James T. B. McCudden
2nd Lt Barclay McPherson   PoW 1 April 18

Lt C. Parry
Capt Phillip B. Prothero
2nd Lt Arthur P. F. Rhys Davids   KIA 27 Oct 17

Lt S. Slingsby
Lt R. H. Sloley   KIA 1 Oct 17
Capt F. O. 'Mongoose' Soden

Lt Eric L. L. Turnbull

Lt Harold 'Jackie' Walkerdine
Lt T. W. White   PoW 27 July 17
2nd Lt Douglas Woodman   KIA 11 March 18
Lt R. Stuart Wortley

Representative Aircraft

S.E.5a A4563/B-6	S.E.5a B37/U
S.E.5 A4850	S.E.5a B183
S.E.5 A4852	S.E.5a B505
S.E.5 A4853	S.E.5a B511
S.E.5 A4854	S.E.5a B527
S.E.5 A4863	S.E.5a B595/W
S.E.5 A4855	S.E.5a B630
S.E.5 A4891/6	S.E.5a B4860
S.E.5 A8898	S.E.5a B4861/F
S.E.5 A8903	S.E.5a B4863/G
S.E.5 A8904	S.E.5a B4885
S.E.5 A8909	S.E.5a B4891
S.E.5 A8934	S.E.5a B8266/Y
S.E.5 A8913/B-2	
S.E.5 A8918/W	S.E.5a C1753
S.E.5 A8919	S.E.5a C5303/X
S.E.5 A8923	S.E.5a C5430/V
S.E.5 A8946	
S.E.5 A89435	S.E.5 E1303/A
	S.E.5 F5611
S.E.5a B1	

CHAPTER 2

Circus to France

While the term 'front' in World War Two could mean a fairly small ground battlefield area, an air front was invariably vast. The Luftwaffe units based on the Channel coast from mid-1940 regarded the long series of air combats with the RAF as a fighting front, which it quickly became when the 'six-week' subjugation of the RAF to pave the way for an invasion of England failed. At the end of 1940 the Germans continued to base fighter forces on forward French airfields, poised, as the RAF had been six months previously, to face new moves by the enemy. The *Kanalkampf* was still raging.

To maintain the pressure on English coastal targets and Allied shipping plying the waters of the Channel, the *Luftwaffe* bomber force kept up daylight sorties on most days when the weather was favourable, but operations were now on a much smaller scale, down to single aircraft on more than one occasion. For its part, the fighter force could afford to resume *Frie Jagd* (free hunt) sorties after 31 October, the Bf 109s generally being released from the restrictions imposed by providing close escort to massed bomber formations.

The last day of October was the date pinpointed by the RAF as the 'official' end of the Battle of Britain. It was known through various sources, but primarily from Ultra intercepts, that Hitler had postponed the invasion indefinitely. No notice of suspension was conveyed to the *Luftwaffe* fighter force, which could now take on British fighters in aerial combat, a task in which it had always excelled, and one that had caused the majority of the RAF losses in the summer.

But now, the defence network could choose when and where its Hurricane and Spitfire squadrons engaged. German fighter sweeps were often ignored, the *Luftwaffe's* purpose being easily recognised for what it was. With the bulk of the *Kampfgeschwaderen* having largely discontinued the daylight offensive, there was no reason to join combat with seasoned enemy fighter pilots and risk losing men and machines pointlessly.

This is not to say that all was quiet over the Channel from October onwards. On some days large-scale air battles developed, but overall a general withdrawal of the *Luftwaffe* from France was under way.

That the situation frustrated those members of the *Jagdflieger* tasked with keeping the pressure on the RAF goes without saying. While the Germans also welcomed some respite from the gruelling summer fighting, the *Gruppen* that remained had to show some results. The ace up the *Luftwaffe's* sleeve was the fighter bomber—if the British defence would only react to direct attacks on

Channel shipping, industrial targets and coastal towns, 'hit and run' raids, albeit on a small scale, would surely bring the RAF up to do battle.

Thus, in the autumn of 1940, Herman Göring had given the go-ahead for the conversion of individual fighter *Staffeln* to *Jabo* (fighter-bomber) units, these becoming an integral part of the *Jagdwaffe's* war against England and, indeed, laying the operational foundations for more specialised formations to use single-seat fighters for ground-attack work throughout the remainder of the war.

While daylight activity fluctuated and dwindled in the autumn and winter months of 1940/41, not least because of the deteriorating weather, RAF Fighter Command flexed its muscles for a cross-Channel offensive of its own. The plan turned into a long and gruelling war of attrition that was to last until the Allied invasion of the continent on 6 June 1944.

Cross-Channel sorties by fighters were not new. A number of forays had already been made by December 1940, but these were mere exploratory probes, sanctioned by an authority no higher than an individual squadron's station commander. What now occupied a good many people was something much more ambitious.

By January 1941 British fighter strength was considerable: the units that had fought in the Battle of Britain had largely been rested and re-equipped. There were 45 day fighter squadrons ready for immediate action, 27 with Hurricanes (mainly Mk. IIs) and 18 with Spitfires (the majority flying Mk. IIs). The bulk of these units was available to 11 Group in south-east England on rotation. Units were drawn from five groups which controlled 23 sector airfields. Taking a rough yardstick of a dozen serviceable aircraft per squadron, this gives a total of at least 540 aircraft, a figure which would very soon rise appreciably as the new year brought more squadrons up to strength and ready for offensive operations. New units were also in the process of forming.

To oppose this burgeoning force, the *Luftwaffe* had but two full *Jagdgeschwaderen*, JG 2 based in western France at Beaumont-le-Roger and Le Havre, and JG 26 dispersed on airfields in north-western France, each with a nominal total of around 90 aircraft. Some of the airfields both *Gruppen* had occupied during the Battle of Britain were found to be less than adequate for intensive fighter operations, even during the summer months, and any period of heavy rain made them all but unusable. Consequently, by December 1940 JG 26 had moved to better bases south of the Somme, and although these, too, were not ideal, the new year saw the *Stab* and III *Gruppe* ensconced at Abbeville, I *Gruppe* at Crecy and II *Gruppe* at Gramont.

In addition, I./JG 1 was formed at De Kooy, Holland, to defend the North Sea coast. All units had late production models of the Bf 109, primarily E-4 and E-7 fighters and their fighter-bomber derivatives.

Most of the aircraft equipping these opposing units were therefore little changed, as far as performance went, from those that had fought the Battle of Britain, apart from the fact that the British machines were about to be armed with cannon that the vast majority had lacked in the summer of 1940. In this respect, the Hurricane and Spitfire quickly reached parity with their German opponents, and, in the Hurricane's case, overhauled the Bf 109E in terms of hitting power. Although the Hawker fighter was considered to be on the point

Right *Cramped and claustrophobic though the cockpit of the Bf 109E may have been to Allied pilots who evaluated it, the 'Emil' and later variants became comfortable and reliable weapons in the hands of hundreds of Luftwaffe Experten, many of whom preferred it to the later and in many ways better Fw 190. An early Bf 109E cockpit with British instrumentation replacing the Revi gunsight for test flying purposes is shown in this view. (IWM)*

Below *Sturdy construction was a prime factor in numerous Hurricanes surviving hits by enemy fire. As shown in this factory construction view, the vital areas are well concentrated in a relatively small area of the airframe, which could otherwise absorb damage with little effect. (Hawker)*

Hurricanes soldiered on into the mid-war years and continued to take the war to the nemy on the continent of Europe. In No. 151 Squadron, Hurricanes were used until June 1941, Mk. I L2005 being coded DZ-D while on that unit's strength. (RAF Museum)

of obsolescence and due for replacement by Spitfires in the majority of day fighter squadrons, this transition took time.

Many Hurricane pilots did not feel at all vulnerable, swearing by the robust construction of their machine which, even if thoroughly 'clobbered' by Bf 109s,

*The Bf 109F had, if anything, even further reduced vision from the cockpit due to armour plate protection behind the pilot's head. Again, though, the Germans used the 'Friedrich' to wreak havoc on enemy formations, many of which were equipped with 'better' aircraft. This machine, captured in North Africa, was one of the first complete examples to fall into Allied hands. Note the bent propeller blades resulting from a controlled forced-landing. (*via Aeroplane Monthly*)*

could still bring them home. A Hurricane was well known to be able to withstand an amazing amount of punishment, more than one aircraft having returned from a scrap with its fabric-covered rear fuselage in tatters from cannon and machine gun fire.

Nevertheless, the Hurricane was an old design, one that retained many features of biplane construction, and although very sound, it was not to be the subject of an extensive modernisation programme. Hawker went on to other more advanced projects, while the home-based squadrons gradually changed over to the Spitfire, which had far greater long-term development potential.

On the German side, there were also individual pilots who preferred to stay with the 'tried and tested' Bf 109E rather than convert to the newer F model which came into service in the spring of 1941. Loyalty to the 'Emil' was quite widespread, and examples were to remain in service for some time to come, although the European theatre was soon to become no place to fly an outmoded aircraft. One criticism of the Bf 109F was that it was under-gunned. Carrying only a centreline cannon and two machine guns in the upper forward fuselage decking, it was an aircraft for the *Experten*—all the pilot had to do was to align the nose on the target and press the firing button, or so the theory went.

Belts of .303 in ammunition being fed into the wing of a Hurricane by a Polish mechanic of No. 306 Squadron at Northolt in 1941. Good as the 'hosepipe' effect of fire from eight guns undoubtedly was at bringing down lightly-armoured bombers during the Battle of Britain, a higher number of kills would have been achieved had cannon been available. For the Fighter Command offensive across the Channel, cannon armament gave the Hurricane a tremendous increase in firepower. (Gen Sikorsky Historical Institute)

This was soon seen to demand too much from the novice, who needed a better spread of fire from wing guns, and, on later model Bf 109Fs and the G-series, wing cannon were re-introduced. The Germans were to find the conflicting requirements of high performance and heavy armament difficult to overcome in the Bf 109, which was designed as a lightweight, agile fighter with the smallest possible airframe. Saddled with heavy guns and ammunition tanks, it became sluggish and slow.

Firepower was only one factor in the equation of success or failure in fighter combat, but the damage inflicted on light airframes, despite the increasingly widespread use of amour protection, had showed cannon to be markedly superior to machine guns. The RAF also believed that any campaign that required strafing of ground targets would be immeasurably boosted by the attacking aircraft carrying cannon.

The British view of the merits of cannon armament had to await its time, as industry had not developed a reliable shell gun that could be mass-produced before the start of the Battle of Britain. Instead, it was wisely decided to fit multiple machine guns which, despite their light weight of fire, were available in quantity. British fighter squadrons had to mark time until late 1940, when the 'back room boys' had overcome the technical difficulties associated with a practical cannon, the 20 mm Hispano. There were various obstacles to be overcome in fitting the large weapon into the wings of fighters, not the least of which was absorbing the recoil, but it was not so much the gun as a reliable feed

The MiG-21 gave North Vietnam increased capability against US aircraft, although some of the top pilots preferred to stay with the tried and trusted MiG-17. In the right hands, the MiG-21 was responsible for a number of US combat losses. (USAF)

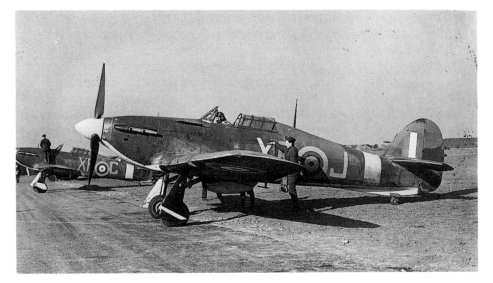

Among the fighter squadrons activated in England in 1941 primarily for offensive ops was No. 71, the first of three Eagle squadrons manned by American personnel. Hurricane Mk. I V7608 is pictured at readiness at Kirton-in-Lindsay, the unit having flown its first sweep from that airfield on 5 February. (IWM)

arrangement that caused the delay.

When the Hispano was mated to British-manufactured adaptations of the French Chatellerault belt feed system, the RAF had a weapon that was to give long and highly reliable service. And once production had geared up, the supply of guns for fighters, initially using ball, incendiary and high explosive (HE) ammunition, did not falter. De Wilde incendiary composition ammunition was introduced in 1941, and this superceded HE shells, which had never proved very effective against armoured structures. The HE/I ammunition proved to be more than adequate, as did the Hispano gun itself.

In this period of transition the RAF embarked on a major cross-Channel offensive, starting in January 1941. To take the war to the enemy and entice the *Luftwaffe* up to fight, various types of operation were devised, each with a codename. The most common were:

Circus—an attack by a small force of light bombers heavily escorted by fighters, operationally limited to the range of the latter and designed primarily to draw the enemy into combat.
Rodeo—a straightforward fighter sweep over enemy territory with no bombers directly involved.
Rhubarb—a small-scale attack by fighters or fighter bombers (often no more than two aircraft) against ground targets, these often being unspecified and left to the prevailing conditions.
Ramrod—an escort similar to a circus, but against more important targets that the bombers were briefed to destroy or at least badly damage.
Ranger—a 'freelance' fighter sweep in varying strength, with the sole object of harrying the enemy.

Rover—an armed reconnaissance behind enemy lines.

Roadstead—an attack by light bombers on shipping or coastal targets under heavy fighter escort.

Unless qualified by a 'Night' prefix, all such operations were flown during the daylight hours—although dismal, low-visibility conditions were often preferred, particularly for Rhubarbs and Rodeos. Targets were chosen carefully, those most sensitive to disruption, such as airfields, industrial complexes, ports and marshalling yards, taking precedence.

Although the number of squadrons and aircraft involved varied, the Circus was the most ambitious of these operations. These were planned and executed by 11 Group, Fighter Command, and utilised 2 Group's light bomber force, then composed almost entirely of the Bristol Blenheim Mk. IV. To ensure that the Blenheims were not unnecessarily exposed to interception, each Circus had at least six elements of fighters:

i) Close escort, which stayed close to the bombers at all times;

ii) Escort cover, which guarded the close escort;

iii) High cover, to prevent enemy fighters penetrating the close and cover escort elements operating at lower altitudes;

iv) Top cover, 'roving commissions' along the bombers' track to prevent any threat, particularly in the target area.

In addition, there were three types of escort flown by elements (usually in Wing strength) independent of the main attacking force and its escort:

v) Target support;

vi) withdrawal cover.

Finally, if it was believed that enemy fighters could be drawn away from the main force, a diversion would be mounted as a seventh element of a typical Circus operation.

The similarity of the Allied fighter offensive to that mounted by the Germans in 1940 was not lost on RAF commanders, nor could its obvious limitations be minimised. Spitfires and Hurricanes had short range, up to 500 miles (Mk. II) and 460 miles (Mk. IIB) respectively, neither being able to fly much beyond Paris on internal fuel with some reserves for combat. Escorting slow light bombers would mean that some pilots would not have much chance to fight if they were to stay close to their charges, and the biggest question of all was whether the *Luftwaffe* would take the bait.

In truth, the British fighter offensive had some significant differences to that of the *Luftwaffe*. The forces sent out were purely tactical, there never being any pretence at playing the kind of quasi-strategic role the *Luftwaffe* had been saddled with in 1940 over England. A great many fighter sorties were intended to do no more than entice the enemy to intercept, and in this respect the RAF could only assume that the Germans would lose more aircraft and pilots than its own squadrons.

Nobody imagined that this would be achieved without some cost to the attacking force, and it was obvious that a pilot shot down or forced to bale out would be lost in almost every case, the embryonic escape network for Allied pilots on the continent notwithstanding. When fighter sweeps began in earnest, the results were not always encouraging. Many pilots thought the sorties to be a waste of time, particularly when experienced fighter leaders were shot down by the *Jagdflieger* or by the ever-present and usually efficient German flak.

The hazards to low-level sorties in hostile airspace did not end there. Weather played its crucial part, occasionally to the advantage of the attackers. Light single-seat fighters were always at the mercy of the elements, which brought such navigational challenges as ground fog, mist, rain squalls and high winds, not to mention the often perpetual overcast, the notorious European 'clag'.

Unfortunately, it was not uncommon for a pilot and his aircraft simply to disappear if the weather turned particularly nasty. Others lost their way, perhaps mistaking landfalls and sallying off on completely the wrong course until they were forced to put down on the nearest flat ground. Fuel state could quickly become critical if a pilot was forced to 'stooge about' looking for reliable pointers to home. The lucky ones managed to crash land on *terra firma* and became prisoners.

Numerous pilots chose the alternative of ditching in the Channel, and it was sometimes touch and go that an individual would be rescued by his own side if a friendly vessel was not in his area. Early in 1941 RAF fighter pilots had not been issued with dinghies, and relying solely on a Mae West was a less than welcome prospect, even for a strong swimmer. For their part, the squadrons maintained patrols over downed comrades as long as they could, and in many cases the rescue services did manage to pluck the unfortunate pilot out of the 'drink'.

By no means an uncommon risk was that of collision. On a large-scale operation, with scores, if not hundreds, of aircraft milling around in a relatively small area of sky, running into a friendly fighter or, indeed, an enemy aircraft during combat, was an ever-present possibility.

If the effort was at times highly frustrating from the RAF viewpoint, some sort of fighter offensive had to be maintained. The aircraft of 2 Group needed employment, and Bomber Command leaders felt it was vital to support the incursions into enemy airspace at night, to deny the enemy the use of Channel waters to move war materials, to disrupt the flow of supplies on rail and road routes and oblige the Germans to maintain air force elements in France to counter the RAF offensive when they might have been more effectively employed elsewhere. Any attrition exacted on the *Luftwaffe* in challenging this effort was deemed to be worthwhile.

For their part the *Jagdfleiger*, now partially tasked with *Jabo* sorties, turned from constantly flying the 'London race track', the regular cross-Channel run to the outskirts of the British capital, to the novelty of hauling bombs. The novelty quickly wore off. To most of the pilots, the very idea of hanging bombs on their Messerschmitts, which had been expertly tuned to get the best possible performance out of what was a less than highly streamlined airframe, was sheer anathema. They knew that, if the RAF put in any appearance before their bombs had been released, they would have little choice but to jettison their loads in order to fight on anything like equal terms.

Because they had not undergone any specialised training and their aircraft had no extra equipment to assist bomb aiming, the exercise certainly had question-able tactical value. In time the techniques would improve, but initially sorties were made at high altitude and the bombs, either a single (550 lb) SC 250 250 kg or four 50 kg (110 lb) SC 50 bombs, all of them carried under the belly of the Bf 109, were released in horizontal flight or a shallow dive.

As almost everyone had predicted, the results were not very encouraging. About the only consolation to the German fighter-bomber pilots was the fact that they were often able to complete their sorties unmolested by British fighters. By keeping low, 'under the radar', they were relatively safe. Unless defending fighters happened to be airborne at the right place at the right time, the Germans would streak in, bomb and be away before the defences could react. Although their efforts often represented little more than indiscriminate 'nuisance raids' the German fighter bombers continued their sorties against England.

Behind the scenes, the British, too, were working on modifications to enable

Although marginally 'cleaner' than that of the Hurricane, the Spitfire cockpit was not exactly luxurious. In this factory view, most of the instrumentation and primary controls have been fitted, items such as a floorpan and fairings not being part of the design. (Vickers)

the Hurricane and Spitfire to carry bombs and other ground-attack stores, but the debut of the RAF fighter-bomber lay some time in the future as Circus Number One was launched, on 10 January 1941.

Weeks of bad weather had meant that this inaugural large-scale operation had been postponed until the first day bringing suitable conditions. The circus, built around an attack by six Blenheims of 114 Squadron, was massive, involving the largest number of RAF fighters put into the air for an operation up to that time. The target was an ammunition dump in the Foret de Guines, south of Calais. The bombers were supported by an impressive force of fighters, individual machines being flown by the cream of Fighter Command. There were three squadrons of Hurricanes (Nos. 56, 242 and 249) which made up the North Weald Wing commanded by Sqn Ldr Victor Beamish, plus three of Spitfires (Nos. 41, 64 and 611) comprising the Hornchurch Wing, led by Wg Cdr Harry Broadhurst. Withdrawal support was provided by a further three Spitfire squadrons, Nos. 66, 74 and 92 of the Biggin Hill Wing, led by the redoubtable 'Sailor' Malan, with Sqn Ldr Johnnie Kent leading No. 92. In total, the fighter force numbered 103 aircraft, 72 of which provided the main bomber support force.

Getting under way in the early afternoon, the fighter force assembled over Southend and the Hurricanes of 242 and 249 squadrons, led respectively by Sqn Ldr Douglas Bader and Sqn Ldr R. A. Barton, maintained a height of 10,000–11,000 ft over the Channel, sweeping ahead of the Blenheims flying

Meanwhile in France ... The Luftwaffe *carefully marshalled its slim fighter resources to combat incursions by the RAF. With numerous* Staffeln *rotated home for rest and re-equipping after the Channel Front operations of 1940, the Germans found themselves in a position not unlike that of the RAF the previous summer. They, too, had to choose which targets offered the best return for the risk of taking on superior odds. In this view, ground crews and an Italian officer use muscle power to push the 7,000 lb bulk of a Bf 109F of III./JG2 into its protective hanger at one of the airfields used by the unit in the Cherbourg–Le Havre area. (Bundesarchiv)*

about 1,000 ft above them, the bomber box being protected by 56 Squadron. The Spitfires acted as the top cover, cruising at 13,000–15,000 ft, their formations stepped up and back.

Nearing the enemy coast off Calais, the force turned to make landfall at Gravelines, where the flak opened up ineffectively, the Blenheims diving in company with the close escort to 6,800 ft. At that altitude they released their bombs on the target, starting two fires before they turned for home.

Number 611 Squadron flew north after the Blenheims had bombed to find some trade at Wissant. Sqn Ldr E. R. 'Bitters' Bitmead, the CO, attacked a gun position in the sand dunes north of the village and also sprayed German troops in the streets. The squadron's 'B' Flight maintained top cover while this low-level activity was going on, the strafing having alerted the flak crews.

En route out of the target area the Spitfires were shot at by emplacements at Calais, Gravelines and Sangatte. Fortunately the flak was inaccurate and the fighters were not unduly bothered by four Bf 109s (almost certainly from JG 2) which happened on the scene of action on their doorstep, either by chance or by following vectors supplied by a *Luftwaffe* ground station. These dived towards the tail of No. 611's 'A' Flight, led by Sqn Ldr Douglas Watkins, who turned the flight into the threat. The Bf 109s rolled and dived steeply away, with four Spitfires in hot pursuit. The enemy fighters did not press their attack, and the British pilots re-formed for the flight home.

The two Hurricane squadrons briefed to attack ground targets of opportunity rather than escort the bombers initially found little that made worthwhile targets for their guns. Continuing on, separated from the rest of his unit, Polish pilot Sgt Michael Maciejowski of No. 249 came upon Guines-le-Place airfield. There he found five Henschel Hs 129 observation aircraft parked on the

JG2's French bases, like those of the RAF, had grass runways. Camouflage netting, hardly needed when it was introduced in 1940, took on a new usefulness in 1941 when aircraft dispersed in the open were very much more liable to attack by enemy fighter bombers. In this view, a pilot prepares for a sortie in a Bf 109F previously brought to full operational readiness by the dedicated groundcrew. (Bundesarchiv)

Throughout the war the RAF had more-than-welcome volunteer help from aircrew who had escaped from the continent. It took time to initiate such men into British methods, and it was the autumn of 1940 before squadrons composed almost entirely of foreign nationals were deemed ready for operations. But from 1941 onwards the RAF was a true international force, and among the fighter units was No. 310 Squadron, with Czech personnel. One of the squadron's Spitfire Mk. Vs, EP464, is seen here.

perimeter. He opened fire on these, but two Bf 109s put in an appearance before he had a chance to observe the results. The enemy fighters were at the same height as his Hurricane, so Maciejowski climbed.

At 1,000 ft the Pole opened fire on the nearest Messerschmitt, which promptly turned steeply and dived into a group of trees to become his fourth confirmed victory. It was at about that point that the Hurricane's throttle decided to jam fully open, and, with his engine roaring, Maciejowski had little choice but to make a dash back to Hornchurch. He eventually landed and stopped the runaway Merlin by switching the ignition off.

The rest of 249 Squadron, withdrawing out over the Channel, were fired on by four patrol boats anchored about three miles off Calais. Sqn Ldr Beamish decided to silence them, and went down to rake the vessels with machine-gun fire. The Hurricanes had almost reached the English coast when Plt Off W. M. McConell was attacked by a Bf 109. Wounded by enemy fire, he baled out, the Hurricane ending its days against Dover's resilient chalk cliffs.

Intent on shooting down McConell, the German pilot was himself set upon by Beamish, the big, tough Irishman having turned back to assist. Beamish opened fire, scoring fatal hits on the enemy fighter, which fell into the Channel. The German pilot's own victim had suffered a broken leg and splinter wounds, both of which were attended to in hospital.

Much was learned from this first Circus, but the operation raised numerous questions as to the tactics to employ on future sorties over enemy territory. Some people were all for increasing the size of the bomber force so that selected targets could be hit hard. Many believed that if tactical bombers were to operate at all, the relatively small weight of bombs each aircraft carried might just as well be boosted by a greater number of aircraft. At that time, Blenheim IVs were the most numerous type available to 2 Group squadrons, although supplies of Lend-Lease aircraft such as the Douglas Boston and North American Mitchell were soon to enter the picture.

While increasing the weight of the bombing made a good deal of sense, there was a strict proviso that the bombing leaders should keep their formations tight at all times, maintain prearranged altitudes with no straggling, and make only one pass over the target. Only if these conditions were met could the fighters adequately protect the Blenheims. The knowledge of what Bf109s could do to unescorted light bombers was all too fresh in the memory.

The post mortem on Circus One led to some revision in planning for future operations, but the RAF could really only adapt its operational techniques in relation to the degree of reaction by the enemy. There was no set pattern for Circus operations, although good weather would sometimes see two or three launched on the same day and there were periods when raids were mounted on consecutive days of a given week. As it transpired, the bomber force for Circus operations was not greatly increased, it being quite rare for more than a dozen Blenheims to operate on a single Circus for the remainder of the type's operational lifetime. Even later, 2 Group tended to keep to this number of aircraft for the average Circus.

It was a period of almost continual rotation of RAF squadrons into 11 Group. These units were absorbed into the various wings assigned to the sector stations, and flew an intensive period of operations. Then pilots would be posted away again, for rest or instructor duties, as likely as not leaving their aircraft for the next squadron coming in for a stint in the front line. These movements led both to the renewal of friendships and to the mourning of those

Radiator problems on a Spitfire Mk. V being tended to by Polish groundcrew, probably of No. 303 Squadron at Northolt.

who had succumbed. It was especially sad if the pilots who were lost on offensive ops had come through the gruelling defensive fighting of 1940, although it was inevitable that many Battle of Britain survivors would now be commanding squadrons or wings. There were all too many such sobering occasions for Fighter Command.

In February, No. 92 Squadron received the first cannon-armed Spitfire Mk. Ibs to enter service, closely followed by Mk. Vbs. Across the Channel, one of their chief antagonists left France for a short duration stay in Germany, when JG 26 departed on 9 February. The unit would not return to its old airfields, but occupied new locations on the north-western coast, flying Bf 109Fs from 1 April.

During March a non-operational trip by two *Luftwaffe* officers was to have far-reaching effects on Fighter Command—far greater than the highly welcome addition of heavier armament for the premier British fighter. Reporting for temporary secondment to the Rechlin test centre were *Oberleutnant* Otto Behrens, *Staffelkapitan* of 6./JG 26, and the *Geschwader's* Technical Officer, *Oberleutnant* Karl Borris. Their input to the development of the Focke-Wulf Fw 190 was backed by invaluable combat experience, and with a team of 30 engineers at their disposal the two pilots conducted numerous test flights and generally helped to keep the programme moving along.

The main problem with the prototype Fw 190s lay in inadequate engine cooling and resultant overheating. The addition of an engine cooling fan eventually cured the problem, but this and other defects, at least 50 of them according to German sources, helped keep the new fighter out of front line service for another five months, and it was not until 21 September that pilots of

Numerous fighter squadrons rotated into 11 Group for spells of offensive operations before passing on to other duties and theatres. One such was No. 3 Squadron, which flew daylight sweeps with Hurricane Mk. IICs in the spring of 1941 before reverting to its main forte of night fighting. This aircraft is BD867/QO-Y. (IWM)

Little changed any further, apart from the addition of a tropical filter for use overseas, the Hurricane Mk. IIC represented the zenith of this famous fighter's lineage. Equipped here with flame guards to shield the pilot from exhaust glare at night, BD867/QO-Y is the same No. 3 Squadron machine as seen in the previous photo. (Hawker)

315 (Polish) Squadron came home to report engaging a hitherto unknown radial-engined enemy fighter.

More punch was added to Hurricane squadrons when the first cannon-armed Mk. IIC entered service early in April with No. 3 Squadron, which moved south from Scotland to Martlesham Heath on the 3rd of that month. Although day fighter sweeps were not No. 3's main forte, the advent of the cannon-armed Hurricane gave the aircraft a new lease of life in that role. Other squadrons were to be equipped with it throughout 1941.

Experience did not always count in the air battles that developed over France. This was shown on 9 August, when Douglas Bader went down during Circus 67 to St Omer. Struggling free of his wrecked Spitfire, which had been cut in half by the propeller of the Bf 109 that collided with it, the legless ace only just made it. He was fortunate indeed to be able to leave one of his artificial legs, inextricably trapped, in the doomed fighter.

An idea not only of the pace of fighter operations at this time, but of the cost to the RAF, can be gleaned from some statistics. Over a six-week period in June–July 1941, 123 pilots were posted as missing from sorties involving the loss of 129 aircraft, 14 of them bombers, as a direct result of enemy action. There were 46 separate operations involving more than 8,000 sorties. However, the command appeared to be well and truly achieving one of its primary objectives, that of whittling down *Luftwaffe* strength.

In the same period, fighter pilots filed claims for 322 enemy aircraft destroyed, 110 of these being fighters. These claims, made in good faith and checked as thoroughly as was possible in the circumstances of air combat over enemy territory and surrounding areas of sea, were subsequently seen to have been on the high side, a not unusual occurrence in any air force during the war.

By mid-August 1941 there was visual confirmation that the RAF had gone over from defence to offence, when Fighter Command issued instructions to repaint all fighters in green and grey camouflage, rather than brown and green, from the 21st. While this probably did not mean much at the time—apart from extra work for the long-suffering ground crews—the change did mark a transition that was widely welcomed. Limited in range as the offensive was, and would continue to be, the loss rate on Circuses and other types of sortie remained within acceptable limits.

In succeeding months the composition of RAF squadrons changed, with cannon-armed Spitfire Mk. Vs becoming more numerous. On the 22nd Hitler's armies turned East to attack the Soviet Union, and most British people suspected that the direct threat of invasion was finally over. There was some perceptible stepping-up of Circus operations over the remaining days of the month, with the somewhat optimistic object of taking some of the pressure off the Russians. Seven more were flown, two each on the 23rd and 25th.

A staggeringly fast ground advance supported by the able *Jagdflieger*, who enjoyed an incredible run of victories in the early stages of the Eastern Front campaign, meant little or no immediate change to the strength of the *Luftwaffe* fighter units in the West, although Mussolini's less-than-successful campaign in North Africa did lead to some *Staffeln* being posted to warmer climes. In any event, such was the sporadic nature of the *Jagdwaffe's* response to RAF fighter operations that only a mass denuding of whole *Gruppen* would have been obvious to those flying them. The British interception of German wireless traffic, via the Ultra system, was a reliable source of intelligence on *Luftwaffe* movements, and warning of such action would have been known some time in advance.

On 13 August 1941 a document issued to all RAF units informed aircrew of the existence of a new radial-engined German fighter, but positive identification could not be made at that time. Observations of German airfields by French agents (undoubtedly at some distance and at considerable risk) had apparently

Very costly in men and machines, the RAF fighter offensive was to last 3 ½ years, at least until the invasion in June 1944. Among the hundreds of victims brought down as a combined result of ground fire, enemy fighters, occasional mechanical failure, adverse weather conditions and pilot error, was this Hurricane I, KW-U of No. 615 Squadron. (Bundesarchiv)

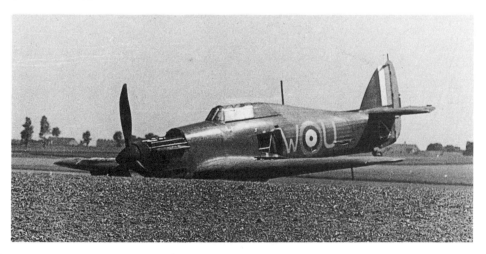

By late 1941 a few of the captured French airfields were reverberating to the roar of BMW radial engines rather than the familiar throaty whine of Daimler-Benz liquid-cooled powerplants, as the Focke-Wulf 190 made its debut. Among the first Staffeln to equip were those of II./JG 1, based in northern Holland. This well-marked Fw 190A, Wr Nr 2125, bears the Tatzelwurm insignia adopted by component Staffeln and marked in the appropriate colour, a neat spiral design on the spinner, and a large winged device below the cockpit. The spiral spinner decoration could be surprisingly effective at close range under full engine revs! (Bundesarchiv)

led to the suggestion that captured examples of the similar-looking Curtiss Hawk had been pressed into German service, leading to a temporary belief in Britain that the new fighter was nothing to worry about. That this surmise was dangerously awry was soon graphically demonstrated. Pilots on the receiving end of an Fw 190 attack could vouch for the fact there was nothing at all obsolescent about this fighter. Most worrying was the fact that, on all counts except tight turns, it appeared superior to the Spitfire V.

It was perhaps fortunate for the RAF that the *Luftwaffe* was not able to throw

Out to grass but poised ready for the next 'Alarmstart' to intercept Allied aircraft is Fw 190A-1 Wr Nr 105 of JG 2's 7.Staffel. White 11 has a vertical I Gruppe bar aft of the fuselage Balkenkreuz. (Bundesarchiv)

Rearming activity was much the same in fighter squadrons the world over, as this group around one of III./JG 2's Fw 190As demonstrates. The eagle's head insignia commonly sported by aircraft of this unit, both as a distinctive emblem and a practical mask for the sometimes heavy staining from the exhaust exit louvres, is clearly shown. (Bundesarchiv)

the Fw 190 wholesale into action against every Circus, Rhubarb, and other operation that was flown. Deliveries of the Fw 190A to first-line units was generally slow, and the winter weather curtailed operations just as JG 26 became the first *Jagdgeschwader* to complete re-equipment with the type, in September 1941.

Somewhat ironically, the RAF credited the Fw 190 with far more capability than its own pilots did. In the early months of service, the A-1 variant continued to be beset by numerous technical problems, some of which manifested themselves only when the aircraft was taxi-ing out for take-off or warming up ready to roll. Incidents such as the one that occurred on 17 September did

The Germans had considerable difficulty in producing external tanks that did not leak, a situation that was marginally worse than no extra fuel at all, as the pilot would believe he had more fuel than was often the case. In this view an Fw 190A-4 Jabo is being given additional offensive capability in the form of a 500 kg bomb. (Bundesarchiv)

nothing to instil confidence in pilots still coming to terms with the Fw 190's very different handling characteristics. From early in its production life the Fw 190A was designed to accommodate a drop tank under the fuselage, a device which the *Luftwaffe* never took to as confidently as did the Allies.

Having survived a belly landing on 12 August, Leutnant Hans Witzel had a Spitfire squarely in his sights on 17 September when a second British machine opened fire from below, hitting the Fw 190's external fuel tank and blowing the machine apart. Among the other early casualties was the II *Gruppe Kommandeur*, Walter Adolph. Flying a two-*Schwarm* sortie on 18 September for a convoy escort, the Focke-Wulfs tangled with the RAF. Adolph did not return, and not until 12 October was his body recovered from the sea.

September and October were unhappy months for JG 26 and on 12 October the fortunes of war came home to the *Luftwaffe* C-in-C. Peter Göring, the *Reichmarschall's* nephew, had recently joined JG 26, persuading his powerful uncle to allow himself and two friends, Wolfgang Ruhdel and Ulrich Dzialas, to stay together at least until their pilot training was completed. Within a matter of weeks, all were united in death.

Ruhdel went down on 17 September, followed by Dzialas on the 21st. Having given his comrade the last rites on 12 October, shortly after his body was recovered from the Channel, Göring took off with Galland that same afternoon for a patrol, acting as the *Kommodore's* wingman. The two German pilots apparently came upon Blenheims flying Circus 108A to Arques and Mazingarbe, charged through the close escort and attacked. Peter Göring opened fire and scored fatal hits on one Blenheim before his aircraft suddenly winged over and spun down into the Channel. It was believed that the Blenheim's turret gunner had hit the Focke-Wulf pilot fatally. When his body

A neat 'finger five' by Spitfire Vs of No. 81 Squadron on a flight over England. Generally losing the edge it had marginally held over the Bf 109, the Mk. V met its match in the Fw 190—but no combat with pilots of equal ability at the controls of their respective fighters was a foregone conclusion.

With the aid of a model, a Luftwaffe *Fw 190 unit commander explains the best tactics for his men to adopt against Allied aircraft. Constant revision of the rules of air fighting had to be made by the Germans as they met a gradually growing number of British and American types, all with different capabilities, armament and (the factor of greatest interest to the* Jagdflieger*) weak points. (Bundesarchiv)*

was recovered Peter Göring found a last resting place beside his friends, in Mareuil-Caubert cemetery.

Despite some German doubts about the Fw 190, there was enough evidence to suggest that the RAF fighter squadrons now needed something a good deal more potent than the Spitfire Mk. V if it was to continue to operate over the continent without prohibitive losses. In the meantime, the squadrons honed their tactics as far as possible while Supermarine and Rolls-Royce worked hard to boost the performance of the basic Spitfire Mk. V airframe. At unit level, it was the view of some commanders that it was long past time to forget tradition, perhaps swallow a little pride and adopt formations very similar to the *Jagdwaffe's* 'finger four'. Leaders such as Sailor Malan put such thinking into practice with positive results. But the spectre of the Focke-Wulf remained very much in the minds of the fighter pilots, who knew full well that the Germans would soon have a good many more of them in service. It was not a comforting thought.

Not that the enemy was exactly left in peace to iron out any teething troubles with its potent new fighter. Airfields were given a high priority in Circus raid planning, and around a third of the 62 operations flown in 1941 were specifically aimed at them. Other targets included marshalling yards, power stations, oil production and storage centres, chemical works and shipyards.

The 'freelance' fighter sorties continued to claim victims, and on 1 November Sqn Ldr Archie McKellar, then leading 605 Squadron, was killed in action. The

Having been the first of the combatant air forces to introduce fighter bombers on any scale, the Luftwaffe was to retain this form of attack until the last months of the war, invariably using different versions of the Fw 190 in the role. In this view an A-4, armed with an SC 500 kg bomb, prepares to taxi out. Note the extensive use of netting to disguise the airfield buildings. (Bundesarchiv)

pendulum swung both ways, however, and five days later JG 26 lost *Hptm Johann* Schmid of III Gruppe, when he was shot down. A further loss to the Geshwader, albeit a happier one, was the departure of Adolf Galland to take up the post of *Inspektor der Jagdflieger*, on 5 December. His replacement as *Kommodore* was Maj Gerhard Schopfel.

For the RAF, 1942 opened on a low note. On 28 January Robert Stanford Tuck was shot down by flak, shortly after returning to operations following a successful tour of the USA. While strafing gun emplacements, Tuck's Spitfire was decisively hit, although the ace was not injured. The news that one of the RAF's top fighter leaders had come down in France resulted in an immediate invitation to dinner with the pilots of JG 26.

Smarting under the disastrous reaction to the daring dash up the English Channel by capital ships of the German Navy, the RAF embarked on another series of Circus operations in 1942. The first took place on 8 March, with a large-scale, four-element attack by 2 Group's new Douglas Bostons. On this occasion the Circus force was sent to Combines power station.

On 28 March another grevious loss was Grp Capt Victor Beamish, the man who had first discovered the *Sharnhorst, Gneisenau* and *Prinz Eugen* boldly sailing up the Channel. Despite his rank, Beamish frequently relinquished the paperwork of command to fly ops, and it was on a sweep over enemy territory that he was shot down and killed.

Spring operations, to a variety of targets, saw the faster Bostons achieving results as good as that of the Blenheim IV, but a Circus still meant a vast effort by the fighter wings to protect them. No such shield was believed to be necessary for another new type, which made its 2 Group debut on 27 May.

Beached on the French coast (and not recovered before the tide came in), Spitfire V AA837 of No. 501 Squadron came to grief on 4 November 1941 after a combat with Bf 109s. (Bundesarchiv)

This, the superlative de Havilland Mosquito, more than lived up to its advance notices—it was still possible to penetrate German airspace without a fighter escort and survive. The 2 Group squadrons lucky enough to re-equip with Mosquitoes never looked back.

The sight of a Spitfire Mk. V lying forlornly in a foreign field became increasingly common as German fighters and flak continued to take their toll. This machine, BL288 of No. 222 Squadron, was posted as missing, presumed ditched in the Channel, after suffering a glycol leak during an escort on 1 May 1942. As shown here, the pilot actually made a dry landing just inland on the French coast. (Bundesarchiv)

Supermarine's approach to Spitfire construction differed markedly from Hawker's methods of building Hurricanes, which was based on earlier design practice. In this view, a Spitfire Mk. IX fuselage shows the degree of completion—right down to the national insignia, tail band and serial—achieved before the complete wing was attached. This was possible because of the development of 'universal' wings, which took a variety of armament combinations and stresses to carry external stores, and could be tailored to various requirements in different theatres of war. (Vickers)

Other units still required the services of Fighter Command, which was itself about to get the boost it needed to fight on equal terms with the Fw 190. Adaptation of the Spitfire Mk. V airframe to take the Merlin 61 engine with a two-stage blower resulted in the Mk. IX, which was first issued to 64 Squadron at Hornchurch in June 1942, the unit being declared operational on the new aircraft late the following month.

Other events made June equally memorable. Despairing of obtaining reliable data as to the performance of the Fw 190, the RAF made somewhat desperate plans to land a small raiding party in France and steal one. To ensure that the purloined fighter got home safely, none other than Supermarine chief test pilot Jeffrey Quill was to fly it. Then, on the 23rd, Oblt Armin Faber of III./JG 2 rendered this highly risky venture unnecessary. Faber, flying a reciprocal course, apparently mistook the Bristol Channel for the English Channel and put his machine down in Pembrey, South Wales, rather than at his home base. Thus the RAF not only had the chance to investigate the nature of the 'poison', but had put the 'antidote' into service within the space of a few weeks.

German fighter units in France remained relatively modest in numerical terms. By July 1942, four *Gruppen*—I and III./JG 2 and I and III./JG 26— had Fw 190As, as did both *Jabo Staffeln* of each *Jagdgeschwaderen*. II *Gruppe* of both units had the Bf 109G. The slow build-up of the Fw 190 was due to a number of teething troubles that manifested themselves as the aircraft began to fly combat sorties. For a time it was touch and go whether the Focke-Wulf's troubles could be cured without major and lengthy redesign. Kurt Tank's engineers worked as hard as their opposite numbers at Supermarine to place a superior fighter in the hands of their flyers.

Undoubtedly because airfield damage could fairly easily be repaired—the weight of bombs dropped never being very high at that stage of the war—the RAF's target emphasis changed in 1942 more towards docks and shipping repair facilities, power stations and rail centres. By early June Morlaix was the only airfield that had been attacked, although 42 Circuses were flown up to 9 May.

Circus raids planned and executed under the jurisdiction of 11 and 12 Groups were not, of course, the only operations flown over France by fighters. Numerous other operations, particularly Rhubarbs, added to the gradual whittling down of *Luftwaffe* strength, although it was a slow process, with RAF losses occasionally being high during a period when the Allies appeared only to be holding the line against the Axis in all war theatres.

Below left The Focke-Wulf fighter had cockpit furnishings that would not look out of place in military aircraft decades in the future. In particular, the side consoles dispensed with the untidy plethora of exposed switches, levers and handles that were a feature of most other first-line fighters of the period, which stemmed from pre-war designs. Shown to advantage here is the 'bridge' of six main flight instrument dials (from left, altimeter, ASI, artificial horizon, rate of climb, compass and engine r.p.m.). The four smaller dials below give oil pressure and temperature, fuel state, and airscrew pitch. Below these is a bomb release panel. (via Aeroplane Monthly*)*

Below right Distinctive rudder markings on Maj Siegfried Schnell's Fw 190 at Thieville, France, in June 1942. Then Staffelkapitan *of 9./JG 2, Schnell scored 62 victories. (Bundesarchiv).*

Fighter Command's war, limited by short-range aircraft, could make relatively little progress until ground armies could return to French soil, a major undertaking that required a good deal more preparation and equipment than was available in 1942. Nevertheless, the gradually expanding air forces based in the British Isles were building an invaluable fund of experience that would be put to good use when the time came. Losses continued to include both experienced veterans and newcomers alike, one pilot definitely in the former category being Wg Cdr Brendan 'Paddy' Finucane. As he returned from a sweep on 15 July, his aircraft was hit by ground fire and dropped into the sea. It apparently sank so rapidly that the Irish ace had no chance to get out, and was drowned.

In August 1942, an invasion 'dress rehearsal' at Dieppe proved how disastrous a full-scale invasion of the continent of Europe might be if the Allies were not fully prepared with overwhelming force at their disposal. Always tenacious and superbly equipped, the Germans grimly demonstrated the folly of such an action with a force inferior to that of the defenders. In the air, the fighter umbrella over Dieppe could only be of limited value, and the outcome of the large-scale air combats that developed during Operation Jubilee was not encouraging. Of the 108 RAF aircraft destroyed, 88 were Spitfires. The Germans admitted to losing just 12 Fw 190s and 2 Bf 109s.

After Dieppe there was not another Circus until 27 August, when Abbeville airfield was the target. Thereafter, until the end of the year, the RAF mounted nine such operations, all of which had shipping and related installations as their targets, except Circus 237 on 1 November, when the 2 Group bombers hit St Omer/Longuesse airfield. Weather conditions did not allow for any further Circus raids until 1 January 1943.

For the German fighter units based in the West the nature of the war had changed radically two days before Dieppe. On the 17th, the first USAAF heavy bombers had made a limited penetration raid on Rouen-Sotteville rail yards, and from these small beginnings grew a mighty armada of heavy bombers that was to be instrumental in the eventual annihilation of the *Jagdwaffe*. Although they hardly realised it at the time, for the Germans the writing was on the wall. They now had to contend with 2 Group operating modern bombers in a 12,000 to 14,000 ft-altitude corridor between the light and heavy flak; Mosquito raids at heights up to 25,000 ft and American B-17s and B-24s at 32,000 to 38,000 ft.

Below all this daylight activity, the Germans were frequently subjected to 'zero feet' strafing and bombing by fighters, not to mention a growing night intruder offensive designed to sap the physical strength of aircrew when they were trying to sleep. More and more responsibility was to fall on the *Jagdflieger* to blunt the Allied air assault that at first threatened the German hold on occupied Europe and then spread inexorably to the very heart of the Third Reich itself. It took another eighteen months to prove that, once committed to the task of liberation, the Allied air forces were not to be stopped.

CHAPTER 3

Pineapple Peashooters

As far as World War Two's disputed Pacific islands were concerned, Iwo Jima was not quite the worst in terms of human life sacrificed to secure a change of occupancy. But the fight for Iwo is probably remembered because it came at a time when the war was all but won, and Japan's demise was all but a foregone conclusion. Even before that volcanic dot in the middle of the vast ocean was finally wrested from the Japanese, Associated Press photographer Joe Rosenthal took an incredible picture of the Marines raising the flag on Mount Suribachi. That image probably conveyed a greater impression of impending victory than thousands of other still photographs.

Although subsequently overshadowed by the carnage of Okinawa, the battle for Iwo Jima was, like most of the campaigns within a campaign that hallmarked the Pacific war, a struggle for airfields—airfields close enough to pound the Japanese Empire into submission with a heavy bomber force of unprecedented power and size. But in this case the island was not primarily seized for bombers, but for fighters.

As with most military operations, a job like Iwo altered in perspective according to an individual's task. A Marine sent to storm Japan's penultimate island fortress against fanatically dedicated opposition would have an entirely different view of the place than, say, an Army fighter pilot. Probably, though, our Marine would almost certainly have preferred the risk of ground fighting to that of flying a tiny little fighter with one engine all the way to the enemy homeland over an awful lot of ocean. Equally, there were few fighter pilots who would have changed places with the guys on the ground, despite the undoubted risks involved in their own job.

By August 1944 the islands of Guam, Saipan and Tinian in the Marianas had been secured, and frantic efforts went ahead to transform modest Japanese airstrips into full-blown air bases capable of accommodating five wings of Boeing B-29 Superfortresses. The pace and scale of the work is reflected in the fact that the first Superfortress shakedown sorties were flown in October of the same year.

In the early days of XXI Bomber Command's existence, the B-29 was not given fighter escort—nor was it very practical to do so, for the distances flown by the bombers from bases in India, China, and later the Pacific islands, were prohibitive, even if large numbers of fighters had been available. The Empire missions involved a 1,300-mile round trip from the Marianas to Japan.

But as B-29 losses began to mount, not only from flak and fighters, but from attacks on the Marianas by Japanese aircraft based on Iwo Jima, it became an increasingly attractive proposition to seize Iwo, despite the fact that this was originally not in the overall strategic plan for continuing conduct of the Pacific war.

Another factor that made Iwo's capture a desirable proposition was its location—almost halfway between the Marianas and Japan. This alone was important, as B-29s that would otherwise be forced to ditch, having run out of fuel or suffered damage, would have a 'halfway house' only 650 miles from enemy targets. It would also eliminate the need for the bombers to detour around the island's defences while it was still in Japanese hands. Equally important was the fact that the enemy would be denied early warning of B-29 strikes by his Iwo-based radar. Above all, an American-held Iwo would make fighter escort to the B-29s practicable.

The combined air and sea operation to take Iwo Jima began on 19 February 1945. Planners had estimated that the island would be secure in four weeks, and by 16 March all serious resistance ended. Partially-cleared areas were used by aircraft as early as February, and an important contribution was thus made by the fighters of the 7th Air Force, spearheaded by the 15th Fighter Group.

Consisting of the 45th, 47th and 78th Fighter Squadrons, the 15th Group had led something of a fragmentary existence. Its personnel had been among the first Americans to find themselves in the front line on 7 December 1941, and pilots subsequently flew numerous defensive patrols over the Hawaiian islands, awaiting a Japanese invasion that never materialised. As the war moved even further from Hawaiian shores the 45th saw some action from Baker Island, Nanumea, Abemama and Makin in the Gilberts from August 1943 to March 1944. The 78th was briefly based on Midway for three months at the beginning of 1943, while the 47th remained in Hawaii. All three squadrons were reunited at Bellows Field, Hawaii, in June 1944.

Otherwise, the 15th trained pilots for service with other groups, transitioning from the P-36 with which it had scored victories over Pearl Harbor, through the P-39 Airacobra, P-40 Warhawk and P-47 Thunderbolt. When Thunderbolts were exchanged for Mustangs in November 1944, with indicators that preparations should be made for a move to a combat zone, it seemed that at long last the group would see some action as an entity before the war ended.

Some men remained sceptical. Ground crewmen bemoaned the need to learn the intricacies of another liquid-cooled engine after the P-47's big radial, but the pilots knew that, if they were going to fight, the long-range P-51 was undoubtedly the best ship for the job.

Training and simulated combat flying continued from Bellows Field while transition was made to the Mustang. The 15th and other fighter units of the 7th, the self-styled 'Pineapple Air Force', initiated an intensive flying training programme which, as the hours piled up, exacted a significant attrition rate. Even as the overseas alert came, accidents and pilot fatalities continued to occur, events made all the more tragic when the 15th's long-serving members were the victims.

Christmas 1944 came and went, and most of January 1945, and still nobody knew exactly where the group was headed. It seemed that the sceptics had been right all along. Combat for the 15th was only a rumour. In the meantime, everyone got used to operating the P-51 and the waiting period was put to good use. It was reasoned that, wherever the 15th was bound, a certain amount of flying over the sea would be necessary, and to increase a pilot's chances of surviving a ditching, Capt Jim Tapp of the 78th Squadron devised a rescue kit built into a 110 gal underwing tank. Comprising an A-3 liferaft, a Gibson Girl radio, rations, and a Navy kit of visual signal equipment, the package went into a kapok bag which served as a liner for the drop tank. Attached to the P-51 wing rack in the normal way, it was triggered by the bomb release. When it fell, a static line pulled open a QA-3 chest parachute and whipped the survival kit out of the tank. After successful tests, the rescue kit tank was assembled in quantity at the Hickam Air Depot and issued to front-line P-51 squadrons. A Mustang so equipped was code named 'Josephine'.

Further work was required to fit a new IFF (Identification Friend or Foe) transponder into each P-51, or at least to make it more accessible for servicing. As delivered, the transponder was very difficult to get at, and 15th Group mechanics relocated it behind the pilot's head armour in place of the battery. The latter was moved to a new location above and behind the engine, a modification that, while it shifted the P-51D's centre of gravity forward slightly, had no detrimental effect on its flying characteristics—in fact, pilots swore that they improved.

Another important modification, which Seventh Fighter Command regarded as the most important of the war as far as its own operations were concerned, was the installation of a second VHF aerial on each Mustang's rear fuselage. The two aerials were tuned to one quarter of a wavelength apart. When a transmission was picked up, one of the aerials would transmit it to the pilot's headphones and suppress the other signal, the right-hand aerial giving the Morse Code letter 'U-Uncle' (dot-dot-dash). The left hand aerial gave the letter 'D-Dog' (dash-dot-dot). All the pilot had to do was to turn in the appropriate direction and refine the heading by watching his magnetic compass. When both signals were received simultaneously, the pilot heard a steady hum, indicating that he was on course for home base or a transmitting aircraft.

It appears that installation of the second aerial was a job carried out when the 15th Group reached Guam and Iwo Jima; not before. Its P-51Ds were certainly delivered as standard 'single aerial' machines drawn from late production D-25 and subsequent production blocks. By 1945 the final D models incorporated many improvements as a result of combat experience, and were undoubtedly among the finest piston-engined fighters in the world.

Then, in late January, it was official. The Japanese were still fighting, and the 15th would have a chance to participate in the AAF's last rounds against the Empire. The delivery of terrain models of the Bonin and Volcano Islands to Bellows Field on 21 January bore testimony to the eventual combat location of the group, but not until 82 P-51s were safely stowed aboard the *USS Sitkoh Bay*, en route for Saipan, were the sceptics finally convinced.

As the mini fleet ploughed across the Pacific, the risk that it would come into contact with the Japanese Navy was remote. Even so, two P-51s were hooked to the Jeep carrier's catapults, just in case. Pilots who would fly off to defend the carrier in the event of an attack were none too keen on the prospect. With the bulk of the 15th's Mustangs occupying much of the deck in four rows, there was no way that they could land back aboard.

No action materialised, and the 15th arrived off Guam on 13 February. Cranes hoisted the fighters off the carrier and on to barges, and they were shipped to the island, to be towed to Orote Field for preparation to fly to East Field on Saipan. There, many members of the 15th met old friends in the 318th Fighter Group, then equipped with P-38 Lightnings.

The officers and men of the 15th had not all been accommodated in the *Sitkoh Bay*, and two transports did not arrive in the area until 19 February—D-Day off Iwo Jima. The AAF personnel thus had a ringside seat of the pre-invasion bombardment of the island, and few believed that anything could have survived the storm of shells and bombs that at times obscured the entire island from view. Unfortunately they were wrong.

As Japanese resistance took its toll of the Marines, the 15th Group's transports were pressed into service as hospital ships. Five days of hard fighting for Iwo meant that it was 24 February before anyone got ashore, the day after the Marines raised the flag on Mount Suribachi. But the island was by no means totally secure, and the troops were told to keep their heads down.

There followed a period of clearing up and preparing Iwo's Airfield No. 1 to receive fighters. All ranks pitched in to complete the job in record time, living in foxholes and eating nothing but K-rations. Sleep was all but impossible, with round-the-clock Marine 105 mm howitzer fire inexorably pushing the Japanese back to two small pockets around Kitano Point and Tachiiwa Point, on the 'fat end' of the pork chop that Iwo Jima resembled from the air.

On 6 March Maj Gen Mickey Moore, chief of Seventh Fighter Command, led P-51s of the 47th Squadron from Saipan to Iwo. Moore landed first and the rest followed. The third pilot down, Whitey Betner of the 47th Squadron, gave almost the entire island a grandstand view of his ground loop when the tailwheel tyre burst as he touched down.

By 7 March the 15th was more or less installed on Airfield No. 1, since given the callsign 'Agate'. A sign that the enemy was still active was the arrival of the 6th Night Fighter Squadron's P-61s. The Black Widows would see action against nocturnal Japanese aerial forays to Iwo, but for the P-51 pilots the ground war on their own doorstep was of more immediate concern. The first operational sorties were to support the Marines fighting just down the coast. With some of the P-51s carrying a pair of 500 lb bombs, the 15th gave increasingly close air support to the Marine front line, complementing the bombing with strafing runs.

The 15th also ranged out over the smaller islands that stretch out from Iwo Jima towards Japan. Although only partially occupied, the Bonin chain had a few hotspots which the enemy had fortified, particularly Haha Jima and Chichi Jima. The latter, 127 miles from Iwo, had an airfield, deep water anchorage and a seaplane base. Although it had been more or less neutralised by Navy and AAF air attacks, it remained a useful staging point for enemy aircraft flying from the Home Islands.

The 15th's 47th Squadron carried out the first attack on Chichi Jima on the 11th, conducting an all but perfect 17-ship strike, with each aircraft carrying two 500-pounders. A repeat interdiction effort the following day was made by

A March 1945 Marine Corps photograph of the 15th Fighter Group's 47th Fighter Squadron lined up on the still dangerous airfield on Iwo Jima. Waving to the cameraman is 1st Lt Bernard P. Bjorseth, who shared a Zero with 1st Lt Roy June on an escort mission to the Tokyo area on 10 June 1945. (USMC)

the 45th FS, and the 78th followed up on the 13th. In all three raids, although enemy flak was encountered and some Mustangs holed, there were no casualties. A Navy destroyer and two Dumbo rescue PBY amphibians were on station just in case any of the AAF aircraft were forced to ditch.

On 14 March the group flew its last ground-support mission. Armed with 110 gal drop tanks filled with a 'home brew' of 60 per cent diesel oil and 40 per cent aviation fuel plus an instantaneous detonator, the P-51s released their makeshift firebombs from an average height of 25 ft to ensure accuracy against Japanese positions, which were extremely well concealed. The extent of the enemy fortifications on Iwo was incredible, and many of the defenders merely went to earth, defying all US attempts to winkle them out. These diehards were to give the new occupiers of the island considerable trouble for some time to come.

Not the least of the hazards was caused by US firepower; whenever an individual Japanese popped up to a lob a grenade or loose off a burst of fire, it would cause a chain reaction among the sentries. All hell would break loose, and it was advisable to seek the nearest hole until the firing stopped.

The 15th recorded its first fatality in the combat zone on 17 March. Everyone knew it was only a matter of time before that grim milestone would be reached, but it came in an unexpected manner. While on a routine combat air patrol north of Iwo, a flight of 45th Squadron P-51s encountered some bad weather. The Mustangs were soon out of it, but when heads were counted one man was missing. No trace was ever found of pilot or aircraft, despite a search. It was not to be the last time that 'natural causes' would claim victims.

A second P-51 outfit, the 21st Fighter Group, arrived on Iwo on 22 March to share the immediate CAP and ground support task with the 15th. Once again, men of the Seventh Air Force had cause to celebrate with old friends.

On 24 March what had started out as a practice air raid alert turned into the real thing, when up to eight Japanese aircraft attempted to attack the island. Two were shot down by the P-61s, and a third was damaged.

Two days later the Japanese struck again, and this time it was no brief skirmish. Before dawn about 300 enemy troops attacked a camp area occupied by the 21st Group and other units. In a four-hour battle, 44 US servicemen were killed and 88 wounded. While the 15th was not directly involved, some of the casualties in the 21st had formerly been on its strength, and the losses were widely felt. Security was tightened and passwords were rigorously demanded whenever anyone had cause to venture out after dark.

For a time, the 15th took over the operations assigned to the 21st Group,

The fighters were on Iwo Jima to protect the B-29s flying the 'Hirohito Highway' to the Home Islands. This crew commander looks as though he is making sure that his men will not fly the next mission without anything they might need, should the worst happen. (USAAF)

which meant more forays to the outlying islands. At the end of March the 15th flew a practice mission to Saipan which was intended as a shakedown for the forthcoming long-range flights to Japan. It did not go well. Several P-51s from the formation of 48 aborted, and less than half completed the round trip.

As March ended, the number of pilots killed had risen to three, a figure which could have been much higher, considering the amount of opposition the group had encountered from ground fire protecting the various targets it had attacked. In its 25 days on Iwo Jima, the 15th had flown 59 missions.

This statistic galvanised someone into organising R & R to Honolulu for up to three weeks, but leave was not popular at a time when the group looked forward to greater things on the operational side. One man found the attractions of Oahu so boring that he took up knitting dog-tag holders for his buddies!

Early April brought confirmation that the 15th was going to Japan: for the first time, AAF single-seat fighters were to escort B-29s all the way to their targets. The media soon cottoned on to a good story and, for once, the Pacific theatre saw the kind of attention usually reserved for other, more accessible war areas. Reporters and photographers crowded into the still spartan facilities of Agate, writing up stories for *Yank* and the Seventh Air Force newspaper, *Brief*. It was indeed an historic event.

This was the mission that everyone wanted to go on, but, understandably, only the most experienced pilots were selected from both the 15th and 21st Groups. There was considerable disappointment at being left out, and one man, Arden R. Gibson, suffered one of those ironies of war that happened in any theatre. Two days before the inaugural long-range mission he fell victim to the over-enthusiasm of a jumpy sentry.

The big attack of 26 March was still fresh in everyone's mind and on 5 April, Arden recalled:

'A perimeter guard, firing at shadows in the middle of the night, bounced a

A 499th Bomb Group B-29, marked V Square 4, takes off for the Home Islands. Numerous B-29 crews were grateful that Iwo Jima, the 'halfway house' between the Marianas and Japan, was in US hands, even though they might never have cause to use its facilities. (USAAF)

bullet off my head while I was sound asleep in my sack. The resulting skull fracture grounded me from further flying for a year.'

It had taken Arden Gibson two years of training and preparation for combat to reach that sad conclusion.

Fittingly, the first escorted B-29 strike was to be on Tokyo. The flock of bombers for the shepherding P-51s on 7 April was more than 100 B-29s of the 73rd Wing, based on Saipan and briefed to hit Nakajima's No. 11 aircraft engine assembly plant at Musashi. As part of a maximum effort for the day, only the 73rd received fighter escort, the 313th and 314th Wings sending 194 Superforts to bomb the Mitsubishi aero engine plant at Nagoya.

While the heavy bombing campaign against Japan was by that time well into its stride—the Nakajima plant strike (Target No. 357 on the list) was the tenth flown against that particular section of enemy production by the 73rd— establishing a fighter escort force involved a whole new set of operational procedures.

It did not take much imagination to realise that a tiny, single-engined fighter could quite easily disappear without trace if it was damaged, low on fuel or happened to stray off course. It had already happened before the first Very Long Range mission, and a lot closer to home. Even if the pilot radioed his position, the Pacific Ocean was so vast that there would be little likelihood of finding him if aircraft and ships had to be sent out to search after receiving a rescue alert. Therefore, in planning the VLR fighter missions, the Seventh Air Force gave priority to doing as much as possible to ensure that an inbound P-51 could locate Iwo, visually if possible and by basic navigational aids if the island was obscured.

More often than not, the island was hidden from view. It became a common saying that if there was a cloud in the Pacific, Iwo Jima was invariably underneath it. This phenomenon was caused by a combination of surface heat and the pressure of sulphur in the salt-laden air that made Iwo more prone to a covering of cloud than other, non-volcanic islands. At sea level up to about 50 ft, the air was clear, but above that, the island was seemingly fogbound.

To overcome this natural hazard, the AAF installed an early example of a Ground Control Approach set at the end of Airfield One. This provided an instrument approach path within about 100 ft of Mount Suribachi's northwest slope. As the P-51D had only a magnetic compass and instrument panel clock, plus voice communication via one VHF four-channel radio, GCA was a useful locator. The trouble was in persuading pilots to trust it. Many wanted plenty of clear-weather practice approaches before they would put their faith in a voice coming through the soup telling them that they were in line with a runway they simply could not see.

Many pilots found the instrument panel clock as reliable a nav aid as any other. While radios and dynometers could malfunction, navigating on a time lapsed-distance basis could still enable a pilot to find that four-mile-diameter dot in the ocean, even after flying the 600-mile leg from Japan.

If the worst happened and a fighter was forced to ditch, rescue vessels stationed at prearranged positions ensured that, if the pilot did not stray a great distance from his intended course, he stood a good chance of being picked up. The service extended right into Japanese waters.

In seven hours' flying time, the pilot would watch this panel continually, particularly the gauge that showed the P-51's fuel state. But by the time the Seventh Air Force was in a position to mount single-seat fighter escorts from Iwo, the USA had in place a very efficient rescue operation for downed flyers, and few pilots were lost in ditchings.

Air-sea rescue usually consisted of five or six 'way-stations' about 100–125 miles apart, the three nearest to Iwo Jima being destroyers and those nearest to Japan being submarines. At the rally point, a submarine would surface as near to the fighters' exit route as possible, and the P-51s would provide one four-ship flight as air cover. Both destroyers and submarines were able to talk with the fighter pilots by monitoring the P-51s' VHF radio D channel. This service by the Navy was backed up by Dumbo PBY Catalinas and B-17s of the AAF's 5th Emergency Rescue Squadron with airborne lifeboats.

All rescue elements, either ships or aircraft, were given codenames specially selected to be difficult for a Japanese national to pronounce, to eliminate the possiblity of the enemy transmitting spurious signals. Thus 'L', 'R' and other letters would usually be included in names such as 'Playmate' 'Jukebox' and 'Chile Williams'. Each pilot was issued with a map marked with the waypoints and codenames.

To ensure that the 'little friends' joined up with the B-29s assigned to act as navigator ships for them, the individual tail markings of the relevant bombers would also be noted down, as would the single-digit radio call numbers allocated to the bombers that fighters from different groups were supposed to meet during the flight. For example, the 15th Group might be on the lookout for B-29s numbered 4, 5, 6 and so on.

The degree of enemy fighter attacks on the B-29s was impossible to predict, and the fact that XXI Bomber Command had started night raids early in March 1945 and kept losses to a minimum—in fact, in 60 missions since October 1944 these had run to double figures only twice. On numerous occasions during that period the command's heavy bomber crews had reported no contact with enemy fighters on some daylight raids, but the claims for Japanese interceptors shot down, damaged or recorded as 'probables' were alternatively high on other days. There was no real pattern to Japanese reaction, although to make any impression at all on the big, well defended bombers, the enemy was obviously obliged, at that stage of the war, to marshall his available forces carefully. The Japanese high command dared not whittle away entirely the means to defend the homeland when the almost inevitable Allied invasion came.

Before dawn on 7 April, many men were up and about on Iwo Jima. Pilots and mechanics fussed over the P-51s, making those time-consuming last-minute adjustments that were part and parcel of every mission, and particularly this one. Nobody, pilot or crew chief alike, wanted an early return because something had been overlooked.

Catholic chaplains held services for men of that faith, the tanks were topped off and the briefing completed. The hands of the clock slowly crawled around to 06:45. Spines tingled as the first Merlin roared into life. Then ten were running, then twenty, fifty, a hundred. The noise reverberated into the calm Pacific morning as Col Jim Beckwith eased his aircraft forward to kick up a characteristic cloud of coral dust. One hundred and seven P-51Ds followed, yellow and black trim identifying the 47th and 78th Squadrons, green and black the 45th.

The take-off went smoothly enough—the gremlins did nothing at that point. They did not wait too much longer, however. As Col Beckwith eased the heavy Mustang out over the ocean, his oxygen was not feeding as it should. There was nothing for it but to turn back. Proving that gremlins are no respectors of rank, Col Moore found that he had problems with a stuck gasoline switch. Elsewhere in the formation, despite all the careful attention to the aircraft before take-off, you could almost hear the pilot's teeth grinding as other Mustangs turned to head back.

Major John Piper of the 47th Squadron took over leadership of the 15th, while Gil Snipes led the 45th and Jim Vande Hey the 78th. The group met its three B-29 navigator ships and followed them to the rendezvous point. The giant formation of silver B-29s was an unforgettable sight, and many of the Mustang pilots were duly impressed. They met up at 18,000 ft over Kozu Shima, less than 100 miles from Tokyo. The lead B-29s were flying at 12,000 ft, with the formation stacked up to 18,000 ft. Having met their charges, the fighter formation had to avoid shooting past them, and pilots began to weave back and forth to maintain their own airspeed and keep the bombers in sight.

As the last of 17 aborts landed back on Iwo, a number of reserve aircraft were sent out as replacements. This was a risky business, for every minute that passed the bombers—and the navigator ships—would be further away. It was solo navigation most of the way for these pilots. One was 2nd Lt Charles C. Heil of the 78th, who flew alone for 600 miles before coming on a formation of Superforts. He joined up with them and flew on, wondering why he could not see any other P-51s. The answer was that Heil had found the 313th and 314th Wings, bound for Nagoya, not Tokyo, and not slated for escort that day. Heil shouldered his big responsibility, glad to have some company.

In the meantime, the main force was approaching Honshu in clear weather. Mount Fujiyama, a familiar enough sight to bomber crews, was a new sight to

B-29s of the 29th Group on Guam. Such was US ascendency over the Japanese by 1945 that the long-range Mustang escorts were relatively few, the fighters' greatest value lying in their ability to destroy enemy fighters on the ground in Japan. (USAAF)

the fighter pilots. At 10:45 the AAF armada crossed the coast of Japan and the first enemy fighters were seen. The Mustangs dropped their wing tanks and prepared to do battle, responding to the numerous reports by the bomber crews of head-on attacks by Japanese interceptors.

The change from drop tanks to internal fuel was always an anxious time. If the switches did not transfer exactly right, the Merlin would stop. Sure enough, it happened to Buck Snipes. As his prop windmilled to a stop Snipes' P-51 lost altitude. The altimeter stopped unwinding at 10,000 ft (he had been up at 18,000) and the Merlin coughed back to life. Maj Snipes and his wingman, 1st Lt Fred Henderson, climbed back to the bombers.

With the ominous bulk of Mount Suribachi dominating the scenery, Mustangs of the 72nd Squadron, 21st Group, await the next call to duty on Iwo Jima early in 1945. (USAAF)

The fuel flow problem also affected one of the most junior 15th Group pilots on the mission, 1st Lt Glenn McCorkle. He was one of the three men in the group which had no previous combat experience, and his element was flying on the 'left shoulder' of the bomber formation at 21,000 ft when the order to release tanks was given. McCorkle takes up the story at that point:

'The P-51s had the external tanks hung on bomb racks, with both electric and manual releases. Evidently, my crew chief tightened my tank sway braces too tightly, because when I pushed the electric release button, the tanks refused to fall. By then the air was full of tanks from the rest of the squadron—so I pulled the manual release cable and away they went. At the same time, my engine quit cold without a sputter.

My tank selector valves were properly set, so I made a turn towards the rally point, which I knew to be out of gliding range. My escape route took me over the B-29s and one obliged me by opening fire and putting a .50 caliber hole in my tail. Meantime, I could hear a lively fight going on over the radio, as the fighters encountered the enemy. Well, at 9,000 ft and alone, I finally discovered that I had accidentally hit my mixture control with my elbow while tugging at the tank release. The Merlin came to life and sounded like a gift from heaven. Of course, I missed a good chance of a scrap because of my misadventure.'

Regarding the 'long legs' of the P-51, McCorkle rates the P-51 as a remarkable aircraft:

'First, cruising at 10,000 ft, 1600 r.p.m. and 34–36 inches Hg, we could maintain about 210 IAS. At this power setting we burned a little less than 40 gal of fuel an hour. We could carry two 80 gal, 120 gal or 165 gal tanks externally, and with the larger ones we always always dropped tanks with gasoline in them.

Internal gas consisted of two 62 gal wing tanks and one 75 gal fuselage tank. The book said not to do aerobatic manoeuvres with a full fuselage tank because it was located so far behind the centre of gravity, causing the plane to be unstable in a high G turn. Nevertheless, we had to do our fighting on the fuselage tank and when that was empty, to get home on the internal wing tanks.'

Other ways to conserve fuel came through experience. Doug Reese of the 45th Squadron recalls:

'On the early missions to Japan, the tanks would be dropped at the landfall. But near the end of the war we waited until we ran the drop tanks dry or were about to fire our guns. Letting your wing tanks run dry was always an interesting experience. You knew when the engine quit and it was a heart-skipper until your engine revived on internal tanks.

Later, we would fly up to and back from Japan at 10,000 ft and switch off our superchargers. To maintain altitude, it was necessary to advance your throttle fully forward. You then increased or decreased your speed to stay in formation using the prop pitch lever. When we got to Japan, we switched the supercharger back in and followed normal flight procedure.'

The Japanese tried to lure the American fighters down low with feint 'juicy' targets. Maj Piper's flight was shadowed by a single low-flying Kawasaki Ki-45 Nick, then four Ki-44 Tojos came in from head-on and broke down and away while still out of range. Recognising the enemy decoys for what they were, the more experienced pilots had to put a tight rein on the combat-hungry young men of the 15th.

But soon the enemy was making firing passes on the B-29s, and dogfights were breaking out all along the fringes of the formation. The opposition was composed mainly of the Kawasaki Ki-45 Nick, the Nakajima Ki-44 Tojo and the latest versions of the Mitubishi A6M Zeke. A lone Mitubishi Ki-45 Dinah reconnaissance aircraft was also reported, but those who saw it and, indeed, shot it down, suspected that the crew had been on a local flight and had stumbled into the B-29s by accident.

Other combats took place all around the bomber formation. Captain Bob Down and 1st Lt Dick Hintermeier, flying as part of Blue Flight of the 47th Squadron, administered a classic 'one-two' punch to a Nick. Down's fire left the enemy fighter's right engine on fire, and Hintermeier followed with more bursts that dealt further damage to the crippled engine and sprayed the canopy. The Nick burst into flames.

Joining with the aircraft flown by 1st Lt Eurich L. Bright, Down and Hintermeier then executed a 180° turn to come in behind a number of Japanese fighters diving through the bomber formation. There was danger in this for the American pilots, as the B-29 gunners were not used to the presence of friendly fighters on their combat sorties, and however good their aircraft recognition, the sheer speed of attacks tended to lace the sky with .50 calibre shells potentially lethal to anyone who flew into them.

When the occupation began, considerable evidence was found that, if the Home Islands had to be invaded, the Japanese would have defended the Empire to the last. Long-range ground attacks on airfields had undoubtedly worn down the enemy, but plenty of intact aeroplanes were found, including this Kawasaki Ki 61 Tony, believed to have belonged to the 26th Sentai, and intended, according to the Marine caption, to be used in the suicide role. (USMC)

On this chase, Down and Hintermeier each flamed a Tojo, while Bright shot down a Kawasaki Ki-6 Tony. A Zeke then passed across Bright's nose. He pressed the trigger again. The Japanese fighter pulled up and then fell away, on fire. Another aircraft, believed to have been a Nick, pulled into Bright's sights and met the same fate. It was last seen falling in flames.

A Nick, intent on the B-29s, either ignored or failed to see the Mustangs flown by Maj Jim Tapp and 1st Lt Paul Maher, who came in on his tail. The Nick pilot soon gave up his attack on the bombers when he went down, damaged by the P-51s' fire. Tapp, climbing to get back to the main scene of action, found a Tony at 20,000 ft. The American opened fire at 800 yd and kept the button down until, he later reported, he was only ten feet away. The Tony took fire and the pilot baled out.

Jim Tapp then saw a Dinah coming at the bombers head-on. Pulling a very tight turn to cut off the fast Japanese twin, he blacked out momentarily. The B-29s were very close, and Tapp abandoned the chase for fear of a collision. This Dinah may well have been the same one observed earlier by Vande Hey, who chased it away. The Dinah's tail gunner fired at him, and Vande Hey's fire tore off its left engine cowling and started a fire. The P-51 turned away when the Dinah went into a spin. It was smoking and apparently out of control.

Another intruder who probably did not realise he had flown into a hornet's nest was an Nakajima C6N Myrt carrier-based reconnaissance aircraft, observed by pilots of the 47th Squadron flying at 15,000 ft ahead of and to the side of the Superforts. Captain Theon B Markham led his flight after the intruder. The Myrt turned into the P-51s, and only Spider Conrick was able to get in a clean shot. The Navy aircraft took two bursts in the wing root and was seen to hit the ground.

Already the value of escort fighters had been more than proved, and as Markham re-formed his flight, he saw high condensation trails as eight Nicks began making unco-ordinated, individual passes on the bombers. As the nearest one approached, Markham fired a long burst and the enemy fighter disintegrated.

On the right flank of the bombers, the 45th Squadron was finding little action, although pilots had seen Japanese fighters making head-on passes and diving through the formation. Some of these runs were too fast to enable the Mustang pilots to draw a bead. Buck Snipes and Fred Henderson finally saw two Tojos at about their altitude, and selected one each. The aircraft at which Snipes fired was hit and fell away smoking as the Mustang overshot, and was lost to sight. Henderson's victim made a sharp 90° turn in front of Snipes, who fired and set it on fire. Snipes saw one of its mainwheel legs drop down and the canopy jettison as the pilot jumped. The canopy barely missed his aircraft. Snipes turned towards the Japanese pilot as his parachute opened, and it occurred to the American that the enemy was probably thinking he had seen his last moments. But Snipes was not prepared to shoot a man in a parachute.

Captain Al Maltby and 1st Lt Wesley E. Brown, who were part of Snipes' Yellow Flight, also found the head-on passes by the Japanese interceptors a little difficult to counter. Maltby's aircraft stalled as he nevertheless got in a good burst at a Tony, which dived away and was soon lost to sight. Wes Brown took off after a twin-engine type (claimed as a Nick) that dropped a phospherous bomb over the B-29s. He caught it and shot it down in flames.

As the Japanese pilots' head-on firing passes brought them quickly out through the rear of the formation, there were many P-51s waiting for them. But the 'dead zone' directly behind the Superfortresses tails was not the healthiest place to be, as Glenn McCorkle had realised earlier. Back at Iwo Jima, he found that the friendly fire had nearly severed his rudder cable.

Near the front of the formation, the fast interceptor passes were doing their best to avoid the aircraft of the 78th Squadron, and it was not until the Japanese mainland at Choshi Point was reached that a chance to score came. Capt Todd Moore, leading a flight at 22,000 ft, spotted several enemy aircraft approaching the bombers below the Mustangs.

Moore's wingman that day was Bob Roseberry, flying his first mission with any action. He saw four Hamps performing lazy eights in loose formation over the B-29s. Sticking close to his leader, Roseberry followed Moore as he closed on the last enemy aircraft. This promptly exploded as the 20° deflection shots struck home. Moore then fired at the No. 3 Hamp. Roseberry was so close to Moore that the Captain's ejected shell casings were striking his aircraft. The target Hamp, 60 ft away, was seen to have most of its underside ripped out. It burned and fell away out of control.

While Roseberry did manage to give the second Hamp in the formation a squirt of fire, he was more concerned with his wingman duty. He observed no hits from his own burst as the two remaining Hamps rolled to come in on the Mustangs. Ignoring them, Moore and Roseberry headed back to the bomber formation, leaving the enemy fighters as though they were standing still. Bob Moore had destroyed two enemy aircraft in 45 seconds.

The P-51 had enough speed at high cruise settings to overtake a Hamp/Zeke at 15–20,000 ft with an advantage of 50 to 100 m.p.h. If he could, the Zeke pilot usually did a split S and went into a dive. The Mustang could usually follow by retarding throttle, because the A6M did not manoeuvre well in a dive. But if it pulled up, or in any way lost speed, it could turn inside a P-51. Provided the leader-wingman element was intact, it was reckoned to be best for the wingman to let the leader take it on. Bob Moore's quick victories proved the point.

Meanwhile, Jim Tapp had his hands full trying to protect a burning B-29 flying directly over Tokyo. He shot down one unidentified two-seater before turning his attention to a six-ship flight of fighters. His fire sent a Tojo spinning crazily down and out of control with six feet of wing gone.

By 11:30 the fury of the air battle had subsided. The B-29s had dumped their loads squarely into the prefecture of the Japanese capital that contained the Nakajima plant, and were heading for the rally point. Post-strike photos would show that that particular production facility was utterly devastated and needed no further attention. Some 300 aircraft had taken part in one of the biggest air battles of the Pacific war. There was still a long way to go before the jubilant fighter pilots could celebrate their victories, and many glanced anxiously to see how much fuel their escort duty had used up. Some regretted having dressed 'as though they were going to the North Pole'. 'Sweating out' the flight back to Iwo took on an uncomfortable reality.

Inevitably, the long overwater flight claimed victims. 1st Lt Frank L. Ayers, covering a single B-29 named *Cyclone Charlie*, had been one of the last to leave

Under glowering skies covering Iwo Jima's South Field, groundcrews of the 15th Fighter Group prepare to attach drop tanks to 78th FS Mustangs on 10 March 1945. Pee Wee and other aircraft carry the bushmaster snake's head badge of the squadron, plus individual names. (USAAF)

the rally point. His P-51 was using fuel a lot faster than it should have done. An hour out of Tokyo Ayers ran into overcast and spent the next 60 minutes flying on instruments. It soon dawned on Ayers that he was not going to make it, and, sure enough, the dreaded fuel warning light soon began to blink. Ayers called up the rescue destroyer that was supposed to be positioned 200 miles off Iwo Jima. He was overjoyed to get an affirmative from the ship, but the overcast persisted and he could not see it. Down to his last few gallons of fuel, Ayers broke out of cloud only 100 ft up—and there was the destroyer. The P-51 responded to a last climb to altitude so that Ayers could make a safe jump, and he floated down. The destroyer had him aboard within minutes.

All of the Mustangs arrived back at Agate between 14:15 and 14:30, after an average 7 hr 35 min, plus about 50 min of combat. Some pilots found that they had only five to eight gallons of fuel left, but there was not a man who would have missed it.

The B-29 crews were generous in their praise at the fine protection they had received. Only three B-29s had gone down, two almost certainly to enemy ground fire. The bomber gunners claimed 80–23–50 (destroyed–damaged–probable), an amazing figure that was, as usual, far too high owing to the number of enemy aircraft sent against them—estimated to be at least 110—and the number of gunners who had fired, often at the same individual target.

One of the most memorable flights was made by Charles Heil. His lone escort sortie to the bombers raiding Nagoya was duly praised, the B-29s even radioing that they would take care of him. Over the target Heil's engine had begun to act up, and he was probably glad of the help. He parried a number of thrusts by enemy fighters and probably at least unnerved a few. Like Heil, they were probably looking for other P-51s.

The 7 April Empire Mission was one of those occasions when everything had fallen into place. Even the weather had been kind and as forecast. Fuel management, perhaps the most worrying aspect as far as the fighter pilots were concerned, was deemed to have been outstanding, and provided a useful yardstick for future escorts from Iwo.

As far as the capabilities of the opposing fighter pilots went, the 15th and 21st Groups had only a nucleus of men who had previously seen combat, and the Japanese can be assumed to have outnumbered the Americans in this respect. And at that stage of the war Japan was fielding some of the best fighters she produced in World War Two. But, as in countless combats since December 1941, the Japanese Army and Navy Air Forces were hampered by aircraft that simply could not absorb hits by multiple .50 calibre bullets. Their propensity to burn often meant that superficial damage became something far more serious, if not fatal. That factor, coupled with intensifying shortages of fuel and most other essential items with which to mount a worthwhile defence, made most air battles seem amazingly one-sided.

The enemy was also sorely tried by the quality and toughness of the primary bomber type carrying out air attacks on the homeland. The B-29, with its modern systems, including remotely-sighted guns, was the toughest proposition any defensive fighter force had to face during the war.

When high-altitude B-29 attacks began, there were few Japanese fighters that could reach them. When the lower-level incendiary strikes were found to be far more profitable, the degree of fighter opposition was potentially far greater, but this did not result in a marked increase in losses to this cause. Japan's lack of a large and well directed night fighter force was also a factor in the success of the Superfortress over the Home Islands, as was the failure to develop efficient radar.

The psychological advantage of attack over defence was also present, as was the eagerness of the Seventh Air Force fighter pilots, not only to meet the enemy, but to do well against him. The fact that the superlative P-51 not only had the range to reach Japan's major cities from Iwo Jima, but to dogfight and strafe airfields and numerous other ground targets, was in itself a sobering enough fact for the enemy to have to face.

The AAF fighter pilots also had the not insignificant advantage of enormous confidence in their aircraft. As Doug Reese says:

'The pilots loved the plane. As a squadron, the 45th had been flying the P-47. It was great at 30,000 ft or for ground strafing work, but relatively cumbersome in other situations. I personally felt we had been given a gift with the advent of the Mustang. It was as though someone had personally presented me with a new automobile. In the movie *Empire of the Sun*, the young hero shouts at some Mustangs strafing a nearby airfield, 'P-51—Cadillac of the skies'. I think that's how we all felt.'

Last, but by no means least, weather played a significant part. In the Pacific theatre weather forecasting could almost be likened to soothsaying, for the air could play a number of nasty tricks, sometimes with very little warning. When it was known that jetstream winds could actually stop a B-29 so that it literally

Other long-range Army fighters were in the Pacific along with Mustangs and Lightnings in 1945, notably the mighty P-47N, the ultimate wartime development of the Thunderbolt line. In this view, Lt Urban Drew gets an entirely different perspective on things to that of a few months previously, when he had flown P-51s in Europe with the 361st Group. The aircraft is from the 414th Group's 456th Squadron, with distinctive blue nose and tail trim. (Drew)

hung in the sky, fighter pilots had to be very wary indeed. The watchword was to go around, up or over weather fronts, never through them.

When the air combat claims for 7 April were added up, they came to a very respectable 26–1–5. The lion's share had gone to the 47th FS, with nine, then came the 45th with seven and the 78th with six. The 21st Group had also done well, with seven for its three squadrons. Jim Tapp's four confirmed kills made him the day's most successful pilot, followed by Eurich Bright, with three. Other

Iwo became a popular base, due to its position halfway between the Marianas and Tokyo, and the AAF P-51 contingent soon had company on the penultimate contested island of the Pacific war. On 18 April 1945 the visitors to Iwo included 4th MAW Corsairs en route to the Ryukyus. The PB4Y-2 Privateer in the background may have navigated for the F4U pilots, just as the weather-recon B-29 was undertaking that role for the P-51s lined up in the background. (USMC)

individual scores pushed up the total, and Bob Moore's two Hamps helped him eventually become the top ace of the Seventh Air Force, with 12 victories. John Mitchell of the 15th was second, with 11, and Jim Tapp fourth with eight.

These were losses that the Japanese could ill afford at that critical stage of the war. The 15th Fighter Group received a Distinguished Unit Citation for its work that historic day—a fitting finale to a near-perfect fighter mission in a long, gruelling campaign. Unknown to the pilots of the 15th and other fighter groups poised on that small chunk of volcanic rock in the middle of the Pacific, completing the job would take just four more months.

As things turned out, there were to be only 13 more VLR escort missions to Japan. Fighter strikes to the Empire began on 16 April, and at least 36 more were sent out. Not all were effective because of a number of factors, primarily weather, but the Seventh AF found, just as in other theatres of war, that there was equal or even more value in fighters carrying out ground strafing, rocket and bombing attacks on enemy bases and destroying aircraft on the ground than in waiting for them to attack bomber formations.

While this phase of the Pacific war had similarities with the bomber escort picture in Europe, the relative strengths of the opposing sides differed markedly. In particular, the B-29 needed escort far less than did a formation of B-17s or B-24s, and the ability of the German fighters to absorb battle damage from bomber guns was far superior to that of the Japanese aircraft. There was, of course, the psychological comfort of the little friends, and many a B-29 crewman, then and now, would probably choose to have the fighter escort along.

However, although fighter strikes wore down the enemy even further, such missions were gruelling for the pilots. Seven hours aloft was regarded as routine, and it was not uncommon for this to stretch to another 60 min. The 'worry' factor of navigating over the distances involved imposed more of a strain than was probably fully realised at the time. Even following the navigational B-29s took its physical toll, for such flying was extremely boring and tiring. Pilots resorted to benzedrine tablets to help them remain alert. Another way to take the dullness out of things was to formate with a B-29 and get a tow. This was done by easing into the slipstream of a Superfort and letting aerodynamics do the rest. It was found that, if the fighter pilot slid right in next to the bomber and picked up the propwash from the number three engine, a properly-trimmed P-51 could sit there, almost locked in place.

Such close escort enabled the occupant of the bomber's right hand blister window to count rivets and generally observe North American metalworking techniques, but the bomber men's natural aversion to fighters—any fighters—that close was often too much of a strain. To bring his crewman's blood pressure back to normal, all the B-29 pilot had to do was change the power setting on No. 3 engine, whereupon the fighter would be ejected from his free ride. This practice might not have been in any flight manual, but it did keep everyone awake.

A standard tour of operations for a P-51 pilot on Iwo Jima was originally established as 15 VLR missions, totalling around 105 hours' flight time, plus as many 'local' ASR patrols and ground support sorties as were necessary. To ensure that a pilot completed his quota, good ground maintenance was paramount. There were few complaints. Iwo Jima's line crews were universally

Sharing Iwo's dusty facilities in 1945 was the 506th FG, one of three with P-51s that flew from the island before the Japanese surrender. Ground crews and pilots of the 458th FS critically note the technique of pilots taking off ahead of their own fighters. (USAAF)

praised, and extra chores such as waxing and polishing the airframe for a few extra m.p.h. were even welcome, simply because it kept men occupied.

When the fighters landed after a mission there would be the usual groundcrew activity to check them over, perhaps patch a few holes and prepare each one for the next sortie. There were jobs that always had to be done. For example, it became routine to change the spark plugs after every VLR mission, as the hours at low r.p.m. cruise settings tended to burn the plugs.

Between 4 March and the end of the war, 2,251 B-29s made emergency landings on Iwo Jima. If each aircraft had the full 11-man crew aboard, that was 24,761 men, a proportion of whom would have been lost if the island had been bypassed, as per the original strategic plan. Understandably, not all emergency landings were accomplished without further injury to the crew or damage to the aircraft, but the fact that Iwo was captured at least saved these crewmen from a soaking when their bomber would have had little alternative but to ditch. There were some nasty accidents and spectacular crashes, such as the time when one battered B-29 careered off the runway into a P-51 flightline and burned, taking a couple of Mustangs with it.

Iwo Jima, described at the time as 'one of the world's most ugly, useful islands', served its time as a base and a haven very well indeed. It undoubtedly

Peace. Lined up on Iwo Jima without fear of any further attention from the enemy, the 21st Fighter Group could pat itself on the collective back for a job well done. The road had been long, but the 'Pineapple Air Force' had been in at the kill. The 21st suffered heavily in the Japanese surprise Banzai attack on Iwo Jima on 26 March 1945. (USAAF)

speeded the demise of the Japanese Empire during those terrible months at the end of World War Two.

Representative aircraft, 15th Fighter Group
P-51D
45th Fighter Squadron (Numbers 51–99)
44-63474/86 *Foxy*
44-63314/54
44-63325/68
44-63465/56
44-63474/86
44-63428/60

47th Fighter Squadron (Numbers 150–199)
44-63395/157
44-63420/176
44-63423/15 *Squirt**
44-63375/168
44-63355/156
44-63423

78th Fighter Squadron (Numbers 100–149)
44-63353/124
44-63441/ *Gloria Beth*
44-72857/122 *Marie U*
44-63407/ *Nina Lou-II*
* Group CO's aircraft used 47th FS markings but with a lower number than any other aircraft.

CHAPTER 4

Honcho over China

With the end of the greatest military struggle the world had ever known, the late 1940s settled into a period of uneasy peace. The term was relative, as small-scale skirmishes, primarily the result of latent nationalism, had begun to develop even before the major warring nations had laid aside their arms. In some areas, peaceful was hardly how the locals would have described their condition. Thus began a long series of 'limited' wars which tended to be only limited in geographical area and the amount of arms available to the participants. The ferocity of the fighting varied, but on the whole these little wars were to involve many nations either directly or indirectly, and were to drag on, sometimes for years, without military or political resolve and, in some cases, to overlap with new outbreaks of violence in other parts of the world.

In the majority of these little wars airpower played its part, and although the major powers drastically cut back orders for new military aircraft, scrapped thousands of those they did have, and demobilised on a huge scale, the fact remained that the world was a far more dangerous place in 1945 than it had been in 1918. The ghosts of the Second World War could not so easily be laid to rest.

The advent of the turbojet as a viable alternative to the piston engine led to a desire on the part of the USA and USSR particularly to build up fleets of jets to form the core of their respective national defence. New bombers, to project power and maintain the peace, were what both sides most urgently needed. The fighter's job would be primarily to defend territory against the incoming hordes. This thinking closely paralleled that of the 'twenties, but with the rider that, if the bombs carried were atomic or nuclear weapons, widespread destruction with appalling after-effects from radiation bordering on annihilation would result. Whether or not the bomber would get through this time was a moot point, but far more was at stake if it did.

Fighter forces also wanted jets, primarily to intercept bombers should the need arise. Fortunately the USA made great strides in this area, keeping pace with its eastern counterpart, which was pushing ahead with adapting new aerodynamic principles to the volume production of modern combat aircraft.

With the creation of the East and West 'superpower' blocs, there was a marked reluctance, particularly by the West, to be drawn into small wars for fear of triggering off the chain reaction of wider conflict. Then, on 25 June 1950, war erupted in Korea.

If the conflict had begun with a series of small-scale actions—as would many others—designed gradually to wear down the meagrely-equipped forces of South Korea, the outcome may well have been different. But a large-scale military invasion by the North Korean Army across the 38th parallel was something to which countries sympathetic to the South could hardly fail to respond. Much of the world was at that time resolved to act unilaterally to 'defend the weak and oppressed' under the auspices of the United Nations (UN).

Wrongly labelled a 'police action' by US president Harry S. Truman, the Korean war became a protracted and bloody affair lasting three years. Truman's unfortunate description was to be widely quoted, leading to the impression that the war was a much more low-key conflict than was the case. His words hardly described accurately the scale of fighting that developed during the first of the 'major' limited wars. Military action to guarantee the shaky democracy of Syngman Rhee's South Korea was conducted under political constraints imposed by the Western powers, ostensibly designed not to offend the great mass of the communist bloc. Even though Red China was the main battlefield adversary of UN forces from late 1950, the 'no-go' areas remained.

These constraints worked through to combat units and made themselves particularly felt by UN flyers, who were banned from attacking targets in Manchuria, on the other side of the Yalu River which bisects Korea and provides a natural demarcation line with China. In 1950 it became the northern barrier of a battlefield. UN rules created sanctuary areas for North Korean and Chinese aircraft when the Yalu was established as the limit of the operational area for aircraft supporting the South.

Although Korea turned out to be the first in which the UN showed true teeth in the spirit of post World War Two agreements, the bulk of the fighting was done by the USA. Initially caught wrong-footed by widespread postwar demobilisation and reduction of forces in its spheres of influence overseas, the USA fed men and material into Korea via bases in Japan.

In the air, the UN had from the start established air superiority in support of ground forces. US Far East Air Forces (FEAF) command, encompassing the assets of the Fifth Air Force, had managed, with few resources, to exploit the fact of the enemy singularly failing to deploy substantial air support to protect his combat troops. The meagre North Korean Air Force was quickly driven from the skies, and consequently the advancing ground forces sustained appalling casualties from round-the-clock air interdiction.

Despite this, the ground situation rapidly became critical as the North Korean People's Army (NKPA) pushed relentlessly south. By August UN forces held only a perimeter of some 40 miles surrounding Pusan and, short of a very dramatic reversal of fortunes, there seemed little left to do but evacuate and leave South Korea to its fate. The reversal came on 15 September, with Gen Douglas MacArthur's masterly invasion at the port of Inchon, some 150 miles behind the North Korean front line.

With substantial UN and Republic of Korea (RoK) forces behind them—a parallel South Korean thrust had been mounted at Yongdok—the NKPA was forced on to the defensive. Retreat became a rout as spirited UN fighting cleared vast areas of enemy troops. Seoul was retaken on 26 September, and by

The late prize. Try as it might, Fifth Air Force failed to get its hands on an intact MiG-15 for evaluation before the Korean armistice was signed in August 1953. When North Korean pilot Ro Kum Suk finally did defect in September, the chance was still taken to test fly the erstwhile enemy's best fighter. Removed to Okinawa, it was flown by a number of pilots, including Chuck Yeager, before eventually being sent to the USA and the Air Force Museum. (USAF)

19 October UN troops were inspecting the damage their own airpower had inflicted on the North Korean capital, Pyongyang. There will perhaps always be debate on whether or not the advance went too far north, but by 25 October RoK forces had reached Choisin, on the Yalu. Suddenly, the retreating enemy was no longer running. The counter-attack came from Chinese troops, a fact few wanted to believe at first. Slowly the reality dawned. China was now the main adversary in Korea.

In the air, too, the appearance of the Russian MiG-15 in late 1950 altered the picture. Here was a very real potential threat from the communist side. Had a serious air challenge to UN forces, spearheaded by the MiGs, been planned and carried through to coincide with the actions of the Chinese People's Volunteer Army (CPVA) on the ground, the outcome might have been disastrous for South Korea. As it was, although the enemy made periodic efforts to wrest back local air superiority, this was never achieved. No cohesive plan appeared to have been implemented by the Chinese or the Russians to support their North Korean allies, who demonstrated little or no understanding of the tactical use of airpower.

As far as ground combat was concerned, the CPVA had very firm ideas of how to achieve superiority. Although it sustained high casualties, its 'human wave' assaults on UN positions were terrifyingly effective, not least by their psychological impact. The creeping paralysis of demoralisation pervaded the UN front line, and a second long retreat down the Korean peninsula began.

It was at this time that the substantial number of MiG-15s that began to appear over Korea represented their greatest threat. Although there was little or no evidence of direct ground support by MiGs, they had the potential to cause serious disruption of the UN air strikes on the advancing Chinese. The UN was forced to respond by sending to the war theatre the one Western jet fighter capable of meeting the MiGs on equal terms.

The fact that the North American F-86 Sabre was the only swept-wing jet fighter available highlights not so much Western slowness in exploiting the advantages of new aerodynamic principles to cope with a new era of flight—numerous such designs had flown and were about to reach volume production—as Russia's speed in taking up the challenge. A great responsibility was therefore placed on the shoulders of USAF Sabre pilots, for there had already been demonstrations of what a well-flown MiG-15 could do against piston-engined aircraft and first-generation straight-wing jets. The situation was indeed serious.

There is little doubt that, had the communist cause followed a workable air plan and used the excellent qualities of the MiG-15 more intelligently, the war might have lasted a good deal longer, with an outcome far worse from the South Korean standpoint. The potential was certainly there. What actually happened was that the F-86 wings found an enemy unsure how to exploit his undoubted advantages and a gradually widening kill ratio—a ratio that was to remain in favour of the American pilots throughout the conflict.

Unlike the situation early in World War Two, US fighter pilots entered combat in Korea with the indisputable advantage of experience. Many individuals had hundreds of hours on jet and piston-engined fighters and were multiple aces from the last war.

While it was rumoured that a number of similarly experienced Red Air Force aces were training the North Koreans and flying missions against the Sabres, the

A fine view of an F-86F of the 336th FIS, 4th Fighter Wing, over Korea, taken by Maj Gene Sommerich from an accompanying Sabre. (Sommerich via Howard Levy)

As in World War Two, the Sabre pilots in Korea did not shrink from personalising the aircraft which they flew regularly, and the 4th Wing had some claim to the practice, as it had been the first F-86 Wing in the combat zone. Angel Face & the Babes *was the mount of Col Royal 'King' Baker of the 336th FIS. (Via R. L. Ward)*

general standard of communist pilots was low in comparison. On occasions, however, there was no doubt that the MiGs were well led by men who knew their job. These 'honchos', as they were nicknamed, were not positively identified as Russian, Korean or Chinese, but it was not hard to guess that they had gained their experience outside the Land of the Morning Calm.

The first F-86 unit to fly combat missions over Korea was the 4th Fighter Interceptor Wing, under the command of Brig Gen George F. Smith. The Wing, comprising the 334th, 335th and 336th Fighter Interceptor Squadrons

(FIS), had occupied Johnson Air Base in northern Japan from 28 November 1950, having travelled from the USA by sea. The urgency of the situation necessitated the F-86s being embarked aboard the escort carrier *USS Cape Esperance* and stored on the open flightdeck with minimum protection from salt spray. Upon arrival, a period of hard work was necessary to clean off the effects of sea water on each airframe, and it was not until December that flying could begin.

George Smith took 'Detachment A', consisting mainly of aircraft and pilots of the 336th FIS, to Kimpo, where the first orientation flight was made on the 15th. Lieutenant General Earle E. Partridge, then vice-commander of Far East Air Forces, assigned a pure air superiority duty to the 4th: 'to fly combat air patrol over northwestern Korea and to meet, turn back and, if possible, destroy MiGs'.

The mount of the 4th Wing was the F-86A-5, the main production model of the initial Sabre variant. Powered by the General Electric J-47-7 turbojet, the aircraft could attain a maximum speed of 679 m.p.h. at sea level, had a service ceiling of 48,000 ft, and an initial climb rate of 7,470 ft/min.

Although the Sabre was not supersonic, it had an airframe strong enough to withstand the high G forces imposed by combat manoeuvring, and was capable of transonic flight when the occasion demanded. With two 120 gal drop tanks, the range of the F-86A was 330 miles, giving a total average mission time of 1.62 hr.

This performance made the F-86 the West's most advanced interceptor fighter at the time of its service debut. The fact that it had stemmed from the wartime straight-wing XFJ-1 and was a simple, relatively unsophisticated design undoubtedly endeared it to pilots more familiar with the technology of an era that was rapidly passing. The F-86 did not come with a complex range of electronic aids designed to push forward the 'state of the art' and thereby inevitably requiring more lengthy pilot conversion time.

Each of the six Colt Browning M-3 machine guns had a standard load of 267 rounds of ammunition, with a maximum of 300 rounds, the firing rate being 1,100 rounds per minute. Aiming was by an A-1CM lead-computing sight linked to an AN/APG-30 radar located in the upper lip of the fuselage nose air intake. Offering automatic lock-on and target tracking, the radar had a sweep range of up to 3,000 yd.

While it was an excellent aircraft in almost all respects, the F-86 had an Achilles' heel in its limited range—hence the need to base the 4th Wing as near to the front line as possible. Until territory had been secured and an extensive base improvement plan implemented in Korea, only three airfields were even capable of sustaining jet operations: Taegu (K-2), Suwon (K-13) and Kimpo (K-14). Of these, only the last two were close enough to the fighting for Sabre operations to be effective, Taegu being much too far south. As Suwon was already extremely crowded, the 4th Wing had little choice but to make Kimpo its forward base.

If the MiG threat had been put into perspective by the world's first jet-versus-jet combat on 8 November, when an F-80 had despatched one, there was no doubt that the appearance of the modern Russian jets worried the FEAF. The MiG-15 had been designed by an aeronautical bureau well versed in meeting

Slim Pickens for the Dark Horse *was the way one pilot personalised his aircraft, in this case F-86F 51-2829. (Via R. L. Ward)*

fighter aircraft requirements, and its performance was very close to that of the F-86.

Aeronautical history has often demonstrated that a potentially wide margin of superiority does not transmit automatically into fact without some essential and not-so-obvious ingredients. It was certainly true that the MiG had a performance edge on all other fighters in the UN inventory. In particular, its armament of one 37 mm and two 23 mm cannon was heavy compared with the well-proven but far lighter .50 in machine gun that armed the majority of US types at that time, including the F-86. But the fact that the MiG-15 gave little or nothing away to the early F-86A, and in some respects was markedly superior, was not to be the deciding factor. Technical merit is rarely enough on its own to make the difference between victory and defeat.

The biggest difference between the F-86 and MiG-15 force lay in pilot quality and attitude. In both, the 4th Wing held an excellent hand; many of its pilots had already achieved ace status, and all had had better than one year's training at the controls of the F-86. Most important of all, they were very keen to show what they could do in combat with their hot new jet fighters. The necessary aggressive fighter pilot spirit was there in abundance.

The North Koreans, on the other hand, had hardly had much chance to gain experience on jet aircraft of any kind. Otherwise equipped with obsolete Soviet piston-engined fighters and attack bombers, the North Korean Air Force (NKAF) had nevertheless decided to make a quantum leap to the swept-wing MiG. For many individual pilots, sudden orders that they should not only fly their unfamiliar new aircraft on combat missions, but deploy them well enough to turn the tide of an entire war, was a very daunting prospect indeed.

It was not long before the 4th clashed with the MiGs. On the morning of 17 December 1950, Lt Col Bruce Hinton led a flight of the 336th FIS from Kimpo to sweep the area of north-western Korea that became notorious as 'MiG Alley'.

To be on the safe side, Hinton and his colleagues used F-80 callsigns and flight profiles, just to see if the Red pilots would fall for the ruse and think they could score a couple of easy victories. Near Sinuiju a flight of MiGs duly appeared and a short, sharp combat ensued. It ended in victory for the US pilots. Hinton himself shot down a MiG, to become the first F-86 pilot to score a confirmed kill over the potential decider of the Korean air war. Hinton's victory roll over Kimpo signified that perhaps the challenge to UN air superiority was not now as deadly as it had first appeared.

But there was no room for complacency. At that time, details of the MiG-15 were virtually non-existent in the West, and even the US intelligence community was unable to provide answers. Apart from the very remote possibility that an intact example could be captured and flight-tested, F-86 pilots could only estimate its performance when the two types met in combat. What was known was a little sobering, for comparison showed that the MiG was a worthy adversary—sometimes far too much so.

The first large-scale combat involving MiGs and Sabres took place on 22 December, when eight 4th Wing aircraft met 15 MiGs. The result was highly gratifying for the USAF—six MiGs were shot down without loss. American pilots noted that, even if the MiG pilots enjoyed superiority in numbers, they

Squarely in the sights of a Sabre pilot, this MiG-15 is about to lose the race for home over the rugged mountains of Korea. While F-86 pilots came out significantly on top of their potentially dangerous adversaries in terms of air-to-air kills, the North Koreans may have lost even more than the official figures indicate, as verification was often impossible owing to the relatively short endurance of the Sabre. (USAF)

seldom chanced more than one pass on a Sabre flight, and when they did open fire they showed a generally poor standard of marksmanship.

By the end of 1950 the 4th had flown 234 sorties. MiGs had challenged 76 of these and eight had been shot down and two more probably destroyed. For this effort, the wing had lost but one F-86A. On the ground, the US 8th Army began a counter-attack on the west coast of Korea and advanced 12 miles. But such small gains were to have little or no effect on the overall situation.

January 1951 passed with very low-key MiG activity. It was assumed that the losses the North Korean force had suffered had some effect on this, and that the enemy was putting in some extra training time, which on previous showings was certainly needed. A spell of bad weather also played its part in reducing air operations to a minimum. Irrespective of what the weather was doing, the FEAF had troubles enough. January 1951 plunged the UN cause deep in the doldrums, and plans were made to evacuate the entire Fifth Air Force back to Japan.

One of the worst aspects of this phase of the fighting was that nobody really knew the strength of the Chicom armies, or where they were. Even an intensive ten-day aerial photographic reconnaissance of the entire front in late December, yielding over 27,000 aerial photographs, failed to identify significant pockets of troops. Masters of camouflage, the enemy had literally gone to ground.

When the size of the enemy armies was revealed at well over 300,000 men, the UN was forced to admit that all it could really do in Korea from then on was to try to contain this force and hold as much territory as possible, primarily by massive application of superior firepower. When the Reds crossed the Han river early in January, the US prepared to abandon Seoul for a second time. On 2 January the 4th Wing detachment left Kimpo and was reunited at Johnson Air Base. The most surprising aspect of this period was the failure of the Reds to use their airpower in support of their troops, who, despite seemingly inexhaustible reserves of manpower, were showing signs of wavering in the face of UN air attacks, which inflicted terrible casualties.

By the time the MiGs again appeared in force, there was evidence that their stand-down period had been put to good use. UN aircrews had to admit that some spirit had returned to revitalise the MiG units they met in combat. This might have had something to do with the fact that the Sabres were still in Japan, but it was more likely that the Reds were conserving their forces for something bigger than the interception of UN fighter bombers and reconnaissance flights. A massive airfield refurbishment and building programme was being undertaken in North Korea and Manchuria. Something was definitely brewing.

The ground situation remained fluid, but there were signs, soon backed by hard evidence, that the Chinese armies had over-reached their supply lines. Also, the constant pounding from the air had affected the planning of their future offensive operations, and there was evidence of more caution in order to save manpower. Ground and air reconnaissance proved that they had not advanced at anything like the same rate as in 1950, leading the UN to believe that Seoul could be reoccupied in the near future.

One of the most urgent needs was to get Sabres back in Korea, but the immediate requirement now was for every available aircraft to be used on ground attack to stem the North Korean advance and to prevent the communist airfield programme being completed. Accordingly, a small detachment of 4th Wing aircraft returned to Taegu on 14 January to fly sorties in the fighter-bomber role, although it quickly became apparent that the F-86A was not the ideal ground-attack aircraft.

Taegu's days as an operational base were numbered (albeit temporarily), as the communists were still on the offensive, and by the 26th the base had been left in the hands of a refuelling and rearming detachment. That same day the US 8th Army began an offensive of its own, designed primarily to secure the vital airfields.

Suwon was back in UN hands by the end of January, and ten days into February Kimpo also changed hands, for the last time. The 334th FIS returned to Taegu on 22 February and, although the base was too far away from the target areas, there was little choice but to use it for the time being. Sabres based there could just reach Pyongyang.

This was the period when FEAF needed F-86s to fly high cover to B-29 medium-bomber attacks on the bases the communists were feverishly attempting to keep open for a suspected offensive. To achieve this, the Superfortresses needed close escort of F-84s or F-80s, both of which had proved well able to deal with the hesitant and indecisive attacks made against the piston-engined bombers. It was when the MiGs were flown by determined, aggressive pilots who would plunge through the close escort to get at the bombers that a high cover of Sabres was very welcome. These occasions were mercifully rare, but MiGs did get through to destroy or damage a number of B-29s. When Sabres were around, it was invariably the Reds who sustained the casualties.

Bomb scarred and battered, Suwon was in a terrible state, but it was the only airfield within range of the Yalu, which is where the Sabres had to be effective. There was no other choice but to try. On 6 March the 334th began to fly into MiG Alley by using Suwon as a staging base. Hairy take-offs were made from the narrow runway as work went ahead to make the place habitable. In four days the 334th was ensconsed there, allowing the 336th to occupy Taegu. This squadron moved up on 6 April, the 334th returning to Japan to be replaced in Korea by the 335th.

The ability of the FEAF to fly into MiG Alley again came none too soon; this was a time when the enemy fighters were at their most aggressive. They were also seen to be flying more intelligent formations, increasing their previously used fluid four to six machines, and while this necessitated a sharp lookout when such formations broke up into pairs and singles for combat, MiGs still fell to the guns of the F-86s in disproportionate numbers.

Meanwhile, the Fifth Air Force maintained its round-the-clock interdiction of enemy airfields, the upshot being that the expected communist air offensive never materialised. There was an attempted strike by Il-10s, which were decimated before they reached their target, and Po-2 biplanes were used to make small-scale nocturnal 'nuisance' raids on Korean bases, but the MiGs did not appear in any numbers over South Korea as had been feared.

They did, however, continue to harass FEAF bomber strikes, but even then the interception rate fluctuated wildly, both in the number of aircraft deployed and the ability (or will) of the pilots to press home attacks. As soon as the Sabres returned to their Yalu patrols, the Americans noted once more than the MiG

Christine and Elenore are the dual names given to this F-86E, 51-2735. Some of the seven and a half visible kills belong to Maj William Whisner, seventh ranking jet ace in Korea. His final tally was five and a half. (USAF)

pilots appeared to prefer to avoid combat unless they had a distinct advantage.

On 20 May the USAF was able to announce that Capt James Jabara had become the world's first jet ace after scoring his fourth and fifth victories that day. Jabara, interviewed after this feat, made a few succinct comments about the relative qualities of the F-86A and the MiG-15. In sum, he said that the Sabre needed more power to enable it to climb a lot faster. The MiGs were then easily outstripping the US fighters if it came to a race to the ideal combat altitude of 27,000 ft. This and other first-hand observations from Korean combat were taken on board by North American and improvements were incorporated into subsequent Sabre models. There is little doubt that the early confirmation that an F-86 pilot had scored the coveted five kills spurred the 4th Wing pilots to emulate Jabara. Whether they were young and relatively inexperienced, or old hands with a lot of Second World War flying in their log books, they were eager to test their skills against the MiG force.

In the early days of the Korean war, the USAF Sabre pilots used combat tactics little different to those employed in World War Two. It was found, for example, that an element of four aircraft was again the right size of basic formation to manoeuvre and fight with in combat. Jet formations were split into two leader/wingman elements, the first two aircraft flying ahead of and about 1,000 ft below the other pair. Each wingman, who positioned himself 200–300 ft back and to the side of his leader, watched the rear quarter. Wingmen would seldom fire their guns unless told to do so by the leaders, or if they found themselves out on their own and threatened by enemy aircraft.

When the word came for assignment to combat duty in Korea, the pilots of the 4th Wing implemented some modifications to the basic finger-four to take account of higher jet speeds. Operational technique was established as: take-off

Bearing the distinctive Fifth Air Force black-edged yellow recognition bands on their fuselages and wingtips, these F-86s, probably replacements, demonstrate the battle formation adopted for combat. (North American Aviation)

as flights of four aircraft each, spaced at five-minute intervals; on reaching the combat area, the flights can break down into leader-wingman elements of two, with the proviso that each pair stay together. Sabre flights would normally arrive in the combat area at between 27,000 and 33,000 ft, which put them below contrail height and enabled the higher-flying, vapour-trailing MiG formations to be seen as early as possible. Each flight usually consisted of a leader, who was the most experienced; the number two, who acted as the leader's wingman and was generally the pilot with the least experience; the number three, the second element leader, who came next in the scale of experience; his wingman, who was also fairly new, and so on throughout multiple flights of four aircraft each. It was found that a maximum of 16 aircraft could be realistically controlled by the leader in combat, and the policy of mixing the available talent gave green pilots the chance to develop sharp reflexes and hone themselves to take over as element leaders as quickly as possible.

On sorties from Suwon up into North Korea, the Sabre flights would spread out at the bomb line (the limit of friendly forces' advance) and adopted this formation, which came to be known as the 'fluid four'. It gave a wider and deeper spread of fighters than the finger four, and better allowed for jet performance. It was found, with experience, that gentle turns were required in conjunction with a shallow dive, to keep the speed up.

By far the biggest problem the F-86 pilots faced in Korea was fuel. MiG Alley lay some 200 miles north of Suwon, and this distance left precious little in the tanks for air combat, when consumption invariably rises. Many pilots, at 'bingo' fuel state, sought higher altitude where consumption was less and began a gentle descent back to base. It was also common practice to climb and flame-out, glide for a few miles and then restart the engine for the landing. While this saved fuel, there was a risk that the J57 would refuse to relight.

After a couple of encounters with MiGs—including the very first one—the Sabres were found to suffer a speed disadvantage, primarily because pilots had been advised, first and foremost, to watch their fuel state. When piling on the coal was known to be a life preserver, fuel conservation was quickly put aside, at least in the combat area. Soon the American pilots were maintaining speeds of at least Mach 0.85, and preferably 0.87. Patrol time was consequently reduced from the earlier twenty minutes to ten; the speeds at which combat took place made this the difference between a seeming lifetime when waiting for the MiGs to appear and far too little time if combat had been joined and the ensuing dogfight involved pursuing them for any distance.

It was the MiG pilots themselves which forced this change. They quickly realised that the F-86 was a far more equal adversary than any other UN aircraft they had met in combat, and the communists became adept at playing a waiting game, timing their attacks only when the Sabres had been in the patrol area for some minutes and had used up a good deal of their precious fuel. Diving passes by the MiGs were invariably at maximum speed, and if the Sabres had let their own speed drop they would have been at a distinct disadvantage.

Altitude, as much of it as possible, was reckoned by many pilots to be the key to survival in combat and beating the MiGs, which were invariably met in superior numbers. If the American pilot could be more or less sure that he was too high for the enemy to jump him, he could use this advantage to overcome any performance deficiencies in his aircraft. Also, the F-86A could not really better the MiG-15 in a tight turn, and to try to do so would often result in a stall. In straight and level flight both aircraft were more closely matched, but otherwise the maxim held to be gospel early in World War Two in the Pacific applied. Just as you didn't try to out-turn a Zero in the previous conflict, so it was not very profitable to try to hold the MiG-15 to a turning match in this one.

As regards the weight of fire available to the F-86A and MiG-15, both types of armament had plus and minus factors. While the MiG could inflict fatal damage with very few rounds of cannon shells, they were cranked out at 250 rounds per minute for the single NS-37 and 550 r.p.m. for the twin NS-23s. This slow rate of fire also carried the penalty of trajectory drop and wide dispersal of shot. Although the MiG pilots could open fire at longer ranges, these limitations of their weapons were compounded if the degree of deflection had not been judged very accurately.

In comparison, the F-86A's six 'fifties created a buzz-saw cone of fire, the rounds leaving the barrels at 1,100 r.p.m. There was far less trajectory drop, and although the weight of fire at impact point was lighter than that of cannon, the concentrated rounds could inflict heavy damage at the average 'ideal' bore-sighted range of 1,000 yd. Conversely, there were plenty of reports of MiGs taking heavy machine-gun fire without going down—a great deal depended on where the rounds impacted.

On reaching their patrol area at the Yalu, the Sabres flew up and down the river on the south side. If conditions were clear, the American pilots could easily see MiGs scrambling from their main base complex centred on Antung on the

The finger four was used to good effect in Korea by the Sabre pilots, who noted many and various tactics on the part of the MiG drivers. Some of these were dangerous, but others were merely defensive, depending on the skill of the pilots—which differed markedly throughout the war. (USAF)

west coast. The other airfields were Tat Tung Kau, Takishan and Fen Cheng. They would cruise high in the cold, clear air and calculate the odds they would probably be up against within minutes. To join combat, they had to wait until the North Koreans were ready to do so. The UN embargo on crossing the Yalu, for fear of a major conflict with China, was generally adhered to throughout the war.

To communicate with each other, the 4th Wing F-86 pilots had an eight-channel radio. Two were tactical channels, one allowed the pilot to talk to the airfield control tower, two were reserved for GCA—one each for the 'initial' controller and 'final' controller—and the rest were reserved for a variety of situations, including emergencies. In the first few months of action there were encouragingly few of these as a result of aggressive MiG attacks, and the F-86s continued to score heavily against them.

Equally, there were occasional graphic illustrations of how much of punch the MiGs packed when individual Red pilots got a bead on a Sabre. Maj Glenn Eagleston came back from a sortie on 28 June with a very perforated aircraft. Only three discernible hits had been scored, one with a 37 mm round and two by the 23 mm weapons, but the side of the fuselage was very badly holed. Sabres came back with large chunks missing out of tail surfaces, mute evidence that a few rounds in the right place could do a great deal of damage.

Fortunately, getting an F-86 in their sights long enough to inflict fatal damage was an achievement beyond all but a few MiG-15 drivers. That fact held good until around June, when the North Koreans appeared to have brought

Near miss! A well posed but succinct comment on the lethality of cannon fire from a well-flown and determined MiG-15 pilot, this photograph shows a Sabre's J47 engine after it had been removed from the fighter. (NAA)

over a bunch of guest pilots. These boys knew their stuff. The US pilots also began to observe a great variety of aircraft markings, which although committed to memory and duly logged in reports, failed to offer much of a clue as to who the pilots were, or their nationality. Speculation was rife.

To this day, the exact identity of the individuals and parent units ranged against the 4th and other F-86 wings in Korea remains a mystery. It was later confirmed, however, that from March 1951 the Soviets had begun sending Czech and Polish volunteer pilots, as well as Russian, for three-month tours of duty with the CPAF units. These men were in addition to a substantial cadre of Soviet advisors who had been stationed in Korea since the start of the war.

By mid-1951 UN intelligence estimated that there were 445 MiG-15s available to the North Koreans, compared with 89 F-86s. This imbalance was redressed somewhat in July, when the first examples of the improved F-86E arrived in Japan, but there was no doubt that the enemy was becoming more aggressive. It was obvious that the North Koreans badly needed some form of air support for their ground troops, but, as this did not materialise, the next best choice was for the MiGs to try to reduce the number of UN fighter bombers by attacking them at their lower operating altitudes.

The FEAF had known right from the MiGs' first appearance that the Russian jet fighter could out-perform all other types in its inventory, and in the summer of 1951 this fact continued to be demonstrated on numerous occasions. Now the MiGs tended to avoid the high-altitude skirmishes with the F-86s, and instead penetrated South Korean airspace at low level, made quick hit-and-run passes on FEAF fighter-bombers, and headed back across the Yalu, keeping low. To mask them from observation from above, the upper surfaces of individual MiGs were painted in dark colours.

With the limited number of Sabres (only 44 of the above total were in fact in service with the 4th Wing), the FEAF was hard put to counter such tactics. Another tactic in the MiGs' repertoire was to come in low and zoom up under a Sabre formation, pilots again trying for a quick shoot-down before the surprised American pilots could react. On occasions these tactics worked, and on others the always numerically-superior MiGs would dogfight the F-86s, but the Reds invariably waited until they had a tactical advantage. Even then, they could always run to the sanctuaries on the north side of the Yalu if things got too hot.

In October the FEAF succeeded in obtaining two squadrons of a second Sabre wing, the 51st, for combat in Korea. Again ferried over by Jeep carrier, the aircraft of the 51st boosted the FEAF force to a total of 165 aircraft, 127 of which were available for combat. The extra help was very welcome.

During the winter the MiGs made yet another change to their tactics—one that gave rise to further problems in countering them. These also showed that the North Koreans had finally grasped the fact that their numerical advantage could be exploited. Sabre pilots began to encounter two distinct formations of MiG-15s, both consisting of some 50 to 60 aircraft. One group would patrol the western coastline while the other flew down the centre of North Korea, both elements strung out in long line-astern formations that became known as 'trains'. These trains would stay high, above 35,000 ft, and individual aircraft would break out and drop down to engage the Sabres. When the 'western' and 'central' MiG trains met up, usually over Pyongyang, they began to fly north to their bases across the Yalu. This homeward leg was dangerous, as a large group would drop down to around 12,000 ft, where they would be ideally placed to bounce slower UN aircraft or Sabres low on fuel. As the larger force approached the Yalu, fresh MiGs would meet them to ward off any F-86s that might have been giving chase.

About half of the MiG trains appeared to be made up of inexperienced pilots who rarely, if ever, offered combat. But there were exceptions. These were the 'honchos', the nucleus of sound experience that held the others together. The word 'honcho' is Japanese for 'boss', and in this context it was highly appropriate.

The FEAF was able to announce its fifth and sixth Sabre aces by November 1951, and in December Maj George Davis became the first 'double ace' of the war, with 12 enemy aircraft shot down in the space of three weeks.

At the close of 1951 the scoreboard stood at 130 MiGs destroyed for the loss of 14 F-86s in aerial combat. By then not all the MiG victories had been in the air, for in November the North Koreans had been unwise enough to base a handful of them at Uiju, on the south side of the Yalu. Two 336th FS pilots strafed the base and destroyed four.

It was early 1952 before the 51st Wing was ready to enter combat, and although priority was given to escorting fighter-bombers, the newcomers soon made their presence felt. MiG killing was no longer the exclusive province of the 4th Wing. However, it was to the original Sabre wing in Korea that the lion's share of the MiG victories was to go. More aces were made during the spring months, the 51st Wing now figuring in the ever-growing FEAF list. Combat victories were corroborated by gun camera film and eye witnesses, and many pilots, although convinced that their quarry could not have made it home in a damaged, smoking MiG, were forced to accept that there was a slight possibility of this if the target was lost from sight, and had to be satisfied with a 'damaged' or a 'probable'. As has been said before, only the North Koreans knew the true figures, and they have never released any details.

Both Sabre wings found the MiG force enjoying a respite during the summer months of 1952. Numerous patrols failed to make contact, or even to see MiGs. For June, the scoreboard read just 20 claimed, down from an April high of 44. Even a maximum effort on the part of FEAF could not draw the MiGs into combat. On 23 June 208 fighter-bombers drawn from USAF, Marine, Navy, RAAF and RoK squadrons attacked the Suiho hydro-electric complex on the Yalu. It was one of the largest air strikes of the war. To screen it, the 4th and 51st Wings put up 108 F-86s, and pilots noted 193 MiG-15s at Antung, some 50 miles from Suiho. The charge of adrenalin many of the Sabre pilots felt as they saw the MiGs taxi out quickly evaporated when it was realised that the enemy fighters were not heading their way but north, away from the FEAF incursions into Manchuria.

June ended with one of the lowest flight-time records ever by the F-86 force. During the following month the 4th Wing passed the last of its F-86A models to care and maintenance and took delivery of enough E models to equip the wing fully.

Outwardly similar to the F-86A, the E model introduced the first of a series of progressive updates of the Sabre. The 'all-flying' tail, in which the elevators and horizontal tail surfaces were linked and moved hydraulically, was the most significant, for it cured undesirable compressibility effects and afforded greater control response when the pilot moved the stick. Valves actuated by control column movement eliminated the need for trim tabs, as trim was automatically adjusted by stick movement. To give the pilot some 'feel' during tail surface movement, an artificial bungee system was provided.

Although the F-86 was the USAF's principal interceptor, the production line had a lot of customers, and even combat units in Korea had to wait their turn in the queue. Consequently, the availability of 60 F-86E-6s, built by Canadair as Sabre Mk. 2s and fitted with US equipment, was very welcome, but examples did not reach Korea until mid-1952.

When combat reports from Korea were studied, it very quickly became clear that the biggest improvement to the Sabre would be obtained by fitting an appreciably more powerful engine. This would hopefully eliminate the relatively slow time-to-climb of the A model, and, coupled with a revised wing design, give improved manoeuvrability. To achieve better performance, North American planned to install the 5,910 lb-thrust J47-GE-27 in the next Sabre model, the F-86F. After some delays in delivery of the new engines, made up by building the F-86E-10 with the J47-13 engine, F-86F-1 production was initiated in the spring of 1952. Examples were shipped to Korea to re-equip the 4th Wing that September. Among the changes made in the F-86E-10 was the introduction of a flat windscreen to replace the 'V' windscreen of the A model, and a revised instrument panel layout. These features carried over to the F

Maj Chuck Owens flew this F-86F, Clan Girl *and* El Diablo. *Eight MiG kills appear under the cockpit, as well as 14 trucks accounted for by this 336th FIS machine. (Via R. L. Ward)*

model, which had a top speed of 604 m.p.h. at 35,000 ft, an initial climb rate of 9,300 ft/min, and a service ceiling of 48,000 ft. Initially the A-1CM gunsight was installed, but the F-10 model introduced the simpler A-4 sight linked to the same gun-ranging radar as earlier models.

Despite the generally lower level of MiG activity, US pilots were still racking up kills. One pilot who flew with the 336th FIS was Captain, later Major, Robinson Risner. He scored his first MiG kill on 5 August 1952, and was an ace by 15 September. Another fell to his guns on 22 October. Number seven came on 4 December, but this one was atypical as far as the quality of his opponent went. In fact, Risner said this MiG pilot was the best he had come across in Korea, American or otherwise.

The mission on which this remarkable combat took place started as a close escort to fighter-bombers briefed to knock out a chemical plant near Sinuiju. It was one of those occasions when the Yalu did not represent an impenetrable barrier. To protect the strike force, the 336th Squadron executed a 360° turn to put the Sabres between the fighter-bombers and the potential MiG threat. The turn took the F-86Fs over the Antung Air University.

Suddenly, there were MiGs in front. Four of them, head-on. Both the Sabre and MiG flights dropped wing tanks, but the Reds were clearly not eager to fight. Risner and his colleagues saw them depart after making a smart 180 in the direction of Fen Cheng airfield. But the MiGs often tried to fool the Sabre pilots into thinking they had quit, only to reverse and try to intercept the slower fighter-bombers at a lower altitude, with the Sabres out of position. Risner watched the departing MiGs just in case they did this. It was vital not to lose sight of the enemy fighters if an interception of friendlies was to be prevented, and Risner (John Red Lead) and his wingman (Red Two) stayed on their tails.

Sure enough, the MiGs showed signs that this was what they intended. Risner maintained the pursuit and caught up with the MiG flight, getting the tail-end Charlie in his sights: the F-86F's radar sight could 'lock on' to the target aircraft and automatically read off the range. Although he was at maximum, Risner fired a short burst.

Sparkling shards of Perspex in the air told Risner that the long-range burst had hit home and given the MiG pilot a very draughty combat environment, if he stayed to fight in that condition. It appeared as though he would, for the MiG turned in to the pursuing Sabres while the rest of the enemy fighter flight executed a descending turn to the right. Risner told Red 3 and 4 to concentrate on the others while he and Red 2 went after the aircraft that had been hit.

The MiG came on hard at Risner, who promptly turned inside it. Risner rolled out and passed within 1,500 ft of the MiG:

'I pulled the nose down and gave him another short burst. It sparkled him a little bit. When I did, he did a half roll and hung upside down, then did a complete roll and ended upside down again.'

As they jockeyed for a good firing position, the three fighters were gradually descending, their speed about Mach .95. The ground was getting a little close for comfort, but the MiG obviously wanted even less air under his wings. He rolled again and started a split S, still going down. Risner thought the MiG was already too low, and that he would not pull out. He widened his own turn to give himself a bit more height, and waited for the MiG to impact. Risner called his wingman:

'Two. This is the easiest kill I ever had!'

But this MiG pilot was something else. Whether he knew there was a dry river bed directly below or not, he found it. Risner was astounded to see the MiG recover and zoom along so low that it created a dust storm and actually kicked up small rocks with its exhaust. Risner considered his next move. To shoot the MiG down he would have to get that low. He dived, but there was so much turbulence from the MiG's jet wash that Risner had difficulty holding the Sabre steady. When he saw the F-86 behind him, the MiG pilot would chop his throttle and deploy the speed brakes, forcing the American to overshoot. Risner continues:

'This guy was one fantastic pilot. I would coast up beside him, wingtip to wingtip, and look him right in the eye. When it looked like I was going to overshoot him, I'd pull up, roll over the top and come down on the other side of him. When I did, he'd throw the coal on to it and go into a hard turn, pulling all the Gs he could.

About the time I'd get the pipper on him, he'd push the stick forward and go into an inverted turn, which is extremely difficult and hard on the eyes and body.

I couldn't duplicate that, and would roll into an opposite turn and start to catch him again.

One time he actually flipped upside down, went up the side of a small mountain, over the top and pulled it through down the other side. I was right side up, so when I went over the top I had to do a half roll to go down the other side.

I was having a real difficult time, but I was hitting him occasionally. I had shot away part of his tail, his canopy was missing, and his left side was on fire. He wasn't in very good shape, but he was fighting like a cornered rat.'

Then Risner and the MiG were down in the river bed again. Watching the chase, Risner's No. 2 yelled: 'Hit him, Lead! Get him!'

Risner's thought was: 'Believe me, I'm doing my best'. Again the MiG pilot chopped his throttle and threw his speed brakes out. Risner coasted up again and, to prevent another overshoot, rolled over the top and came down on the MiG's wingtip. Both F-86 and MiG were coasting, their engines idling.

'He looked over at me, raised his hand and shook his fist. I thought: "This is like a movie. This can't be happening!" He had on a leather flying helmet with no oxygen mask. It had evidently been sucked off when I shot his canopy away.

Then he made a 90° turn back to the right. Before I realised what was happening, we went between two hangars! He had led me right into Tak Tung Kau airfield! Red 2 was shouting again: "Lead, they're shooting at us!"

The flak was bursting all around us. In fact you could see the gun barrels flashing because we were right down on the deck, 35 miles inside China! The MiG pilot had gone up and down the river, leading me to the airfield, figuring the flak would chase me off.'

Meanwhile, the MiG pilot seemed to be attempting to land, but had not yet lowered his gear. He was still flying at about 300 kt, so low that his aircraft was blowing dust off the runway. Risner realised he was not low enough to hit the MiG again. He waited for it to pull up or turn:

'When he did, I really hammered him. I blew about four feet off his left wing. It exploded in fire. When that happened, he made a hard right chandelle, then a right turn back down and parallel to the runway. He was probably trying to make it in the grass alongside the runway.

I fired all the rest of my ammunition into him. He levelled off, still doing about 350 kt, touched the ground and came unglued. Little pieces went everywhere.'

Although the MiG was finally down, Risner and his wingman were in a precarious position, over China and low on fuel. They beat a hasty retreat—but the location of Tak Tung Kau meant that their most direct exit route took the two Sabres right over Antung. Intelligence had previously briefed 4th Wing pilots that the estimated number of guns defending the main MiG base in Manchuria was some 250, many of them with radar prediction. Risner and his No. 2 did not count them, but were prepared to believe the quoted figure because the sky was thick with flak as they passed over the base.

Risner's No. 2 took hits in the underside of the aircraft and began to leak fuel. When he had five minutes' fuel remaining, Risner told him to shut down. Lead was going to push his wingman home. This was achieved by nudging the air intake of one aircraft right into the tailpipe of the other. Both F-86s were fairly light by this time, and the duo kept aloft well enough. Risner pushed all the way to the vicinity of Cho-do Island, where rescue forces stood by to pull downed pilots out of the sea. His No. 2 ejected successfully near the island.

Risner landed at K-14 with, as he put it: 'The nose of my bird all boogered up'. The word was that his wingman would be returned to Kimpo on an evening transport flight, but when the aircraft landed Red 2 was not on board. Risner was stunned to hear that his wingman had drowned before the rescue people got to him. It was a sobering finale to one of the epic combats of the Korean war.

The MiG Honcho Risner had finally shot down on 4 December was his seventh kill. He had not had to work quite so hard for the others, and few other pilots found the sort of challenge Risner had done for his number seven. The action had hardly 'been by the book', and was highly uncharacteristic of Sabre versus MiG combat. At that time the enemy had become quite demoralised at losing aircraft so heavily, and FEAF pilots reported on more than one occasion that their very presence so unnerved rookie pilots that they promptly ejected, sometimes without a shot being fired at them.

Robinson Risner's eighth and final victory was achieved on 21 January 1953, making him the 20th ace of the war.

Further expansion of the Sabre force took place early in 1953, but the 4th Wing lived up to its unofficial nickname, 'Fourth but First', by not only remaining in Korea until the end of the war, but staying in the 'ace race'. Not surprisingly the wing returned the highest number of air-to-air victory claims over the MiGs. The relevant figures were: 218.5 for the 335th, 142.5 for the 334th and 116.5 for the 336th. In addition, the 336th was credited with four destroyed on the ground.

By confirming that a total of 38 fighter pilots had attained ace staus during the conflict, the USAF claimed credit for the destruction of 305.5 enemy aircraft. Aces represented less than ten per cent of the total USAF fighter pilots who received credits for downing enemy aircraft, the final tally being 893 in aerial combat alone. No fewer than 841 of these were MiG-15s.

It would be untrue to state categorically that this figure has not been challenged since, and even the Air Force archivists themselves admit that it is now all but impossible to compile a comprehensive credit list based on a re-examination of each claim. Some discrepancies have been found in the monthly returns of claims filed, the most intriguing of which show that in certain weeks the number of credits awarded for victories exceeded the claims.

There remains therefore, some doubt as to how rigorously the FEAF investigated the evidence for each individual victory claim at the time. But even if the overall total of enemy aircraft destroyed should be revised—if not halved as has been suggested—the fact remains that the achievement of the F-86 pilots in nullifying the MiG threat of late 1950 was one of the outstanding feats of the war. Few could argue with that.

Major Risner stayed in the Air Force, his record in Korea standing him in good stead for duty in Vietnam. Assigned to the 335th TFW flying F-105s out of Takhli, Thailand, he became the first living recipient of the Air Force Cross, the second highest US award for valour, when he led a mission against the Thanh Hoa bridge on 1 April 1965. Over North Vietnam, that widely believed element of luck that should accompany every successful combat pilot finally deserted Robbie Risner. He was shot down on 16 September to become a guest of the North Vietnamese, a harrowing experience he fortunately survived.

CHAPTER 5

'An old-fashioned dogfight'

A decade and a half on from Korea, it was a MiG threat that again brought a new generation of American fighter pilots into an Asian war theatre. The air war over North Vietnam had many similarities with the previous conflict, in that Western politicians strove to avoid unduly trying the patience of the major communist powers. This time they were to prove that they had brought the establishment of 'no-go' areas and resultant enemy sanctuaries to a dubiously efficient peak. Once more the USAF fielded a fighter which was the only one really capable of containing the threat posed by a communist air force—and yet again pilots were to meet a restrained, sporadic response on the part of the enemy.

By and large, the comparison of Vietnam with Korea ended there. This time the USA outnumbered a later-generation MiG force many times over, and the defensive capability of the enemy had no parallel in the previous war. Moreover, international support for US military intervention in South Vietnam was nothing like the wholehearted United Nations backing in Korea. In consequence, the USA undertook virtually a private air war north of the 19th parallel, with little to gain at the outset but almost everything to lose at the end.

Airpower was to play a massive and controversial part in the war in South Vietnam, and from 2 March 1965 the USAF began bombing raids into North Vietnam. Rolling Thunder, the most costly and probably most negative air campaign in history, had begun to build up its ponderous and voracious momentum.

By 1965 the USAF Tactical Air Command (TAC) was re-equipping with a radically different kind of fighter, with a two-man crew rather than the traditional one. In this singular detail the McDonnell F-4 Phantom II represented a very big change from previous fighter doctrine—that, and the fact that it was one of the rare instances when the Air Force took into inventory an aircraft designed for the Navy. When F-4 squadrons answered the call to go to Thailand to ward off MiG attacks on Republic F-105 Thunderchief fighter-bombers, the USA was already substantially committed to military support of South Vietnam. Carrying the war into the enemy homeland by conducting air strikes was an increasingly important part of that commitment, a time-honoured way of showing a nation the folly of aggression.

Unfortunately, the North Vietnamese could not have cared less about any traditional or innovative Western way of fighting a war, particularly one utilising

The way it was in the early days. Two F-105s formate on an F-100F Super Sabre during a mission into North Vietnam. The first of the Wild Weasels, the old 'Hun' was not really up to the highly dangerous work of 'coat trailing' for North Vietnamese radar, and the task was taken over by the Thud. Protection for these strike forces was initially provided by Wolfpack Phantoms. (Republic)

airpower. While the USA approached the challenge in its way, the North worked under an entirely different set of rules. Heavily supported by China and Russia in terms of advisors and equipment, North Vietnam's military forces matured rapidly as one of the world's toughest defence networks was built up, virtually from scratch.

Ho Chi Minh's poor country remained relatively small in terms of airpower, but here too it showed that it was an adversary to be reckoned with, notwithstanding the fact that technology had hardly touched it before the war. A graphic illustration of this was the fact that some fighter pilots had not even learned to drive a car before mastering the controls of a trainer and passing quickly on to the MiG-17. The early success achieved by North Vietnamese pilots in intercepting F-105 strikes would be repeated.

When the first F-4s arrived in Thailand, in December 1965, the Phantom was still new to the majority of the Air Force crews who were to take it into combat. These men knew they had an aircraft that was among the world's best, if not *the* best. Endowed with an awesome Mach 2-plus performance and a load-carrying capability second to none, the F-4C was based on the Navy's F-4B and represented the result of a very full test programme that had seen McDonnell-Douglas capture a set of world records soon after the Phantom became a reality.

The Navy was well pleased with the reliability achieved by the F-4B, and the transition to building a version meeting USAF requirements had been made

When the defences of the North allowed it, the F-4s, like F-105s and B-57s before them, flew straight and level, bomb-on-signal sorties, directed by EB-66 Destroyers. The technique was not recommended for crew longevity once the North Vietnamese got its MiG force mobilised. Straight in and out, full power dive bombing became the more normal method of attack. (USAF)

smoothly and with the minimum of changes to the airframe. Like Navy aircraft, Air Force Phantoms relied on an all-missile armament. Built-in guns were weapons of the past, and, in any event, the big fighter's airframe was filled with fuel cells, electronic bays and two huge afterburning J79 turbojets. There was scant room for a gun.

With such a superb fighter to fly, many F-4 Aircraft Commanders and pilots understandably looked upon the Vietnam war as something that would soon be wrapped up. Whatever the enemy did in the air, they could hack it. Had Vietnam been anything approaching the kind of war that had been fought by the USA in the past—politically or militarily—they might well have done so. Paramount among the things that stopped them were the Rules of Engagement (RoE).

When the first MiG Combat Air Patrol (MiGCAP) sorties were flown to shield F-105 strikes from interception, the F-4 crews began to score kills, but to many participants the sorties wasted the potential of the new fighter. The MiGs were down there, sitting on their airfields, and American crews could see them scrambling. A couple of heavy air strikes, timed to catch the North Vietnamese Air Force (NVNAF) at home, would have been devastating. But the US war managers said no. Why cause unnecessary destruction to the resources of a country that was about to give up its avowed reunification of Vietnam by force of arms?

While a somewhat similar situation had occurred in Korea, in that Sabre pilots had champed at the bit to hit off-limits MiG bases in Manchuria, the difference was that the F-4s were over Vietnam itself, and there was no natural barrier, such as the Yalu River had been, to stop them attacking the airfields. What did stop them was the US RoE.

When they could see no valid reason for such decisions, the fighter pilots began to wonder how the nature of war had changed so much without anyone telling them. They felt they had a right to know, their lives were being laid on the line to do a job made impossibly difficult by the dreaded rules. The lines: 'Theirs not to reason why, theirs but to do and die' had been written about a war in the previous century, but they were never more valid than in Vietnam. Dying was exactly what too many American pilots were doing.

Under these crazy conditions, the 8th Tactical Fighter Wing deployed to South East Asia to fly combat missions out of Ubon, Thailand. As the first F-4 Wing in the theatre, the 8th was to carve itself a reputation second to none, despite the restrictions. It emerged from the conflict as the highest-scoring MiG killing outfit in the Air Force, and included among its members some of the most able pilots to see combat in what was an entirely different age of military flying, light years away from any other in terms of aircraft performance alone.

Yet, as many crews found, not everything had changed. The strictures imposed on fighters and the combat scenario North Vietnam represented meant that a crew still had to make positive identification of the enemy, irrespective of what a radar scope indicated. As for those missiles, which had, they were told, buried the fixed fighter gun forever ... the results the F-4 crews were getting with them simply did not bear this out.

The F-4C went into action armed with four Raytheon AIM-7 Sparrow air-to-air missiles, semi-buried in recessed under-fuselage wells. All F-4s except the dedicated reconnaissance versions, irrespective of the branch of service for which they were ordered, were armed with the Sparrow. In the AIM-7D and E versions, used during Rolling Thunder, the maximum range over which a kill was possible was up to 28 miles. Under Semi-Active Radar Homing (SARH) guidance, which means that the missile homes on to radiation reflected or scattered by the target when illuminated by the radar in the attacking aircraft, the AIM-7 was, with this range, considered as a Beyond Visual Range (BVR) weapon. The F-4's APQ-100 radar emitted electromagnetic energy in continuous rather than pulsed waves all the time it was switched on, usually on a constant frequency.

The Sparrow was ejected from its fuselage recess at the moment of motor ignition, to ensure that its forward moveable control 'wings' cleared any airframe obstructions immediately ahead of it, and was steered to the target by the radar receiver built into the nose. If it was guided correctly, the AIM-7 would home in at a speed of around Mach 4, delivering a 66 lb continuous-rod-type warhead. This rod, around which the explosive was wrapped, shattered into some 2,600 lethal fragments on impact. Either direct action (DA)—i.e. impact—or proximity fuzing could be fitted.

For MiGCAP missions, when contact with North Vietnamese fighters was likely, the Sparrows were usually supplemented by the shorter-range heat-seeking Philco-Ford AIM-9 Sidewinder. Vietnam was not a BVR war, and most Sparrow launches had to be well within the missile's maximum flight envelope; it

Another problem was the widely-held belief that missiles, not guns, would be all the F-4 would need to defend itself in combat. Missile reliability fluctuated widely, although the heat-seeking AIM-9 Sidewinder and the radar-guided AIM-7 Sparrow (shown here before loading) were extensively used, the combination being responsible for the majority of F-4 air-to-air kills over Vietnam. (USAF)

was also found to be prone to numerous malfunctions under South East Asian servicing and combat conditions.

For one thing, the handbook stated that an AIM-7 could not be fired if the carrier aircraft was pulling more than 2.5G. As combat manoeuvres in Vietnam routinely exceeded this figure, the resultant low ratio of kills by Sparrows, around ten per cent of firings, is not surprising. An attempt was made to shorten the range in a developed version of the AIM-7E, but the problems tended to persist.

Overall, the far simpler Sidewinder achieved better results in the combat conditions prevailing over Vietnam. Widely reported to have fewer moving parts than the average radio, the AIM-9B had a range of two miles and was the first production model Sidewinder for the Air Force.

The F-4C used an AAA-4 infrared (IR) seeker to detect electromagnetic emissions from a hostile aircraft or to acquire the target on command from the radar. The seeker then told the missile where to look and slaved the AIM-9 seeker head to its own sensor, thus enabling earlier lock-on and firing than was possible using only the uncooled missile IR seeker head.

The seeker was linked to a command guidance circuit, current from which provided audible warning of target lock-on as a low growl in the pilot's headset. This gradually rose in pitch as the range to the target diminished, and changed into a high 'singing' tone. When that was heard, the F-4 crew could be almost certain of a good launch, maintained lock-on and a hit on the target.

In practice, the early AIM-9B often proved superior to the radar-guided AIM-7, but it had limitations. Pilots often found, for example, that they were close enough to deliver the *coup de grâce* to a MiG with gunfire, and yet in the wrong aspect for effective AIM-9 IR lock-on, or that the target had the wrong type of IR-emitting background. The result was often no kill.

Another drawback with the Sidewinder was that it did not like bad weather. Cloud, rain or grey skies drastically reduced the chances of a good lock-on. In sum, it was a missile that worked well if the parent aircraft was flying at high altitude on a clear day with the target preferably dead ahead. Even low altitude could cause the AIM-9 to stray and mis-guide. Naturally, these ideal conditions were not always present.

Even if he still had AAMs left, there was many an F-4 pilot who rued the lack of that old-fashioned cannon, as the early Sidewinders required careful positioning of each aircraft. They were literally heat seekers, which meant they were incapable of manoeuvring if the enemy fighter's exhaust was not right in front, presenting an unavoidable guidance point. Lacking this, many Sidewinders veered off, bent on taking out the sun, bright reflections, or any convenient aircraft exhaust, irrespective of its country of origin.

Before the F-4 had entered Air Force inventory, extensive tests had been made with 20 mm General Electric M-61A1 Vulcan guns which worked on the rotating barrel (six, in this case) 'Gatling' principle, and which were enclosed in streamlined pods intended to be slung from centreline belly and wing stations. Developed primarily for ground strafing rather than aerial combat, the pods had a slight disadvantage in that they tended to vibrate and spread the cone of fire.

Despite their moans about a fighter without a gun, the 8th and other tactical fighter wings gave a good account of themselves against an often elusive enemy. This F-4D, 63-760 of the 479th TFS, dispersed at Ubon in 1967, displays two MiG kills. (Frank MacSorley via R. L. Ward)

At first, the M61A came in a SUU-16 pod with an air-driven winch to spin the mechanism and start the firing sequence. (GE)

Crews had also to get used to allowing for the downthrust angle of the cannon barrel.

Nevertheless, combat units lobbied long and hard to get supplies of these gun pods to the war zone. Although they were not as good as guns built into the airframe, any help they could have in fighting the kind of war that was taking place—not something that was supposed to have happened in the hypothetical 'next war' when the F-4 was still on the drawing board—was welcome.

Deliveries of the SUU-16A to F-4 units began in 1966. The pod held 120 rounds, which were pumped out at a maximum rate of 6,600 rounds per minute, and was fitted with a ram-air turbine which swung out into the

Development led to the SUU-23A pod, which had a different nose cone and a more reliable and convenient electrical actuation system which was fully enclosed by the pod at all times. (GE)

slipstream to provide the necessary power to motorise the loading sequence immediately before firing. The maximum rate of fire was reduced if the carrier aircraft was travelling at less than 400 m.p.h., and the 'external' turbine arrangement induced a degree of drag.

The supply of gun pods was slow at first, and in the meantime crews came to terms with the limitations of AAMs. Apart from having armament specialists check and re-check that circuitry and seeker heads functioned correctly before the aircraft took off, there was little that could be done to prevent malfunctions in the demanding heat of combat. Missiles continued to go astray and require multiple firings to score kills. Many sure victories simply did not happen as a result—the sheer numbers fired in most successful engagements showed that they had not been sufficiently perfected by the mid-1960s, at least not to completely replace guns in fast-manoeuvring, tactical fighters. Most missile programmes of the 1950s had been geared to the destruction of high flying

The front cockpit of the F-4 changed relatively little during the lifetime of the Phantom, this being an F-4E. Normally the Aircraft Commander occupied the front seat with a Pilot in the back. This did not always work well, as the 'guy in back' sometimes had more F-4 flight hours than the AC. Some fighter pilots did not initially take to the two-man crew concept, and the Phantom brought a whole new set of challenges to the USAF. (McDonnell Douglas)

bombers, which were expected to be launched against US strategic targets when the Cold War became hot. Eventually, Vietnam experience was studied closely, and subsequent USAF fighters made room for a built-in gun.

During the years of the Rolling Thunder campaign the 8th Wing provided escort to the two-wing F-105 Thunderchief force that did most of the bomb hauling and handled the Iron Hand anti-radar strikes. The Wolfpack, in the hands of a number of able commanders during the period, had to write the book on tactics in a war unlike any other. Pitted against a gradually escalating defence net, both Thuds and Phantoms took on the North Vietnamese Air Force, with mixed results. But at the end of what might be termed the first phase of the air war against the North, the 8th emerged with an impressive tally of 37.5 kills. One more was added in the 1972 rematch.

Of all the fighter types mentioned in this narrative, the F-4 was far and away the most complex. Its two-man cockpit was to represent something of a watershed in international fighter design, in that it came at the point when the duplicity of old-fashioned instrumentation was about to give way to the increased use of micro-circuitry to present essential flight data and mission inputs in simple graphic image displays. This might be termed the crossover from 'round, separate dial' analog technology to the fully computerised cathode-ray-tube display banks widely used today. Most importantly, from the USAF's point of view, this enabled one man to monitor the systems once again, at least in the 'pure interceptor' role.

In the F-4, however, the multi-role nature of the aircraft's mission demanded not only a high input from on-board computers, but a full-time crew workload to watch everything that was going on. Heeding all the warning inputs and flying the aircraft became simply too demanding a task for one human brain—or so it was believed. This view was not entirely shared by the fighter pilot community, and the Air Force's operational approach to the Phantom was not widely favoured by many of those tasked to fly it.

At first, a Phantom crew consisted of a front-seat Aircraft Commander and a back-seat Pilot, it being reasoned that it was safer to have two rated pilots aboard in the event of trouble, and that the rear-seat man could fly the aircraft home if an emergency incapacitated the AC. In reality, this rarely happened. After some considerable morale problems stemming from the respective rank and experience of each crew member, the USAF introduced a tidier AC-Navigator arrangement.

Once its two-pilot concept had been worked out, the Air Force could do little to alleviate what became a difficult situation. Unlike the Navy, which attempted to keep its F-4 crews together so that they flew as a team as often as possible, the USAF system allowed—indeed encouraged—the switching around of individual crewmen, often without due regard to rank, experience or even the ability of the individual GIB—'Guy in Back'—to do what was required of him. The broad objective of this policy was to spread experience of the two-man fighter cockpit wide, rather than deep. It did not always work as planned.

With a war to fight, the men of the Wolfpack could not let such matters impair their performance. The dangers they faced going North of the 19th parallel required total undivided attention for the duration of the mission. Any criticisms could later be voiced through channels, but individuals had to be circumspect in choosing a sympathetic ear, for the tactical air war involved a lengthy chain of command, and not every link in that chain understood or, it was strongly suspected, cared very much about the problems they faced.

Nevertheless, the F-4 crews did more than their best under the restrictive and occasionally contradictory Rules of Engagement. With the finest fighter in the Western world in their hands, they could often turn a bad situation to their advantage—and the ground people could only dictate the terms of combat so far. When the landing gear came up and the strike force was outbound, the crews were the only arbiters.

By the spring of 1967 the USA had been conducting an air campaign against North Vietnam for a little over two years. In that time the effort expended against the enemy homeland had brought forth next to no reaction as far as any moves towards termination of the fighting in the South was concerned. Both sides were apparently determined to fight on until some sort of satisfactory conclusion could be negotiated and, for the USA, a military victory in the accepted sense of the word began to seem increasingly elusive.

Interspersing missions with periods of stand-down due both to the US desire to demonstrate goodwill by periodic halting of the bombing, and to bad weather, the 8th and other tactical Air Force wings in Thailand had followed their orders and, as permitted, penetrated gradually into the sanctuary areas that the USA had imposed on most of North Vietnam. When the offensive had been planned, the country had been divided up for operational purposes into 'Route Packages'. The higher the number, the more profitable were the targets—with greater and more concentrated defences.

As US impatience mounted in proportion to Hanoi's seeming indifference to escalation of the war on the home front, so the bombing of military targets crept nearer to the capital and the country's principal port of Haiphong. American tactical aircraft were also flying nearer to the buffer zone established between North Vietnam and China.

By early May most of the parameters of the Vietnam air war had been set. The enemy's strength in AAA defence of factories, bridges, canals and a long list of secondary targets was a known factor, as was the increasing use of the SA-2 Guideline surface-to-air missile (SAM). The North Vietnamese Air Force had been met in combat on numerous occasions, and, more often than not, the US fighter pilots had scored kills. In general, the F-4s succeeded in covering the strike forces so that widespread destruction and disruption of supplies and lines of communication had been caused. All too often, though, any effect on the flow of supplies to Viet Cong and North Vietnamese regular forces fighting in the South was only temporary. Very few targets in North Vietnam were visited only once.

In spite of the sophistication of their own aeroplane, the extent—and it had to be ruefully admitted, the capability—of the AAA, and the fearsome presence of the 'flaming telephone pole' SA-2 making an unwelcome air defence debut, this technological war was not too different to those that had gone before. The SAMs were a case in point. The recommended way to avoid being chalked up by some anonymous Vietnamese battery commander as another Imperialist Air Pirate kill was basic. If they saw a SAM coming, the F-4 crew flew their aircraft to the edge of the envelope and, if necessary, way out the

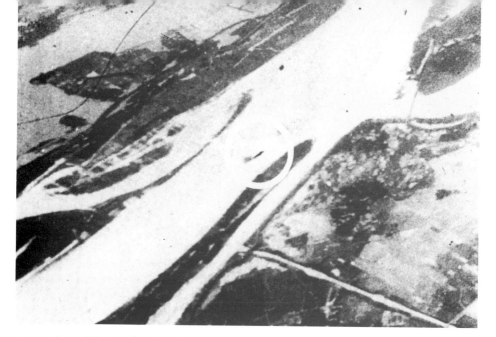

Apart from AAA and MiGs, the third element of the 'triple threat' to US air operations over the North was the Soviet SA-2 surface-to-air missile. If a SAM could be spotted immediately after launch, it could be avoided by combat aircraft, which rarely stopped to take photos. In this case, however, the mission by an RF-4C was to do just that, and an SA-2 launch near the Red River in 1971 was duly recorded. (USAF)

The photo-recon boys often came back with outstandingly clear evidence of North Vietnam's defences, as in this view of three mobile SA-2 launchers and their Fan Song radar and support vehicles. The problem was that such a site could be vacated quickly and appear completely empty and harmless when a strike force returned to knock it out. (USAF)

other side to avoid it. A quick eye and a cool head were what was required, but what usually happened was that the pilot would scream an expletive-laden warning to anyone else in the vicinity and then throw his aircraft all over the sky in a sweat soaked, G-pulling display of survival aerobatics. It often worked, as missiles like the SA-2 were not then capable of turning inside a well-flown F-4. Among the tricks the North Vietnamese pulled was to paint the SA-2 in different colours to match the particular shade of sky on a given day. White was popular, but they also came in black and camouflage brown and green. This the US pilots swore was a good match for the topside shades used on their aircraft.

Definitely more lethal hues told pilots what calibre of AAA was being fired at them, the various colours conveniently denoting the different altitudes each gun could reach. There was black for the deadliest 100 mm; an orange-red core with a black corona indicated 85 mm; white with a dirty grey tinge was 57 mm, and whiter for the 37 mm, and so on. Down low, really low, were the massed ranks of Ho Chi Minh's part-time militias, armed with weapons as modest as carbines but still capable of penetrating a vital part of an airframe. Depending on local organisation and the population of a given region, these civilian defenders could put aside their agricultural implements and be up discharging their weapons at American aircraft in very short order. They did, after all, get plenty of practice.

Heavy calibre anti-aircraft artillery guns tended to be densely concentrated around fairly small targets, and it was widely reported at the time that the flak over North Vietnam could be compared with anything the Germans put up over their cities in World War Two. Vietnam participants refuted this. The Vietnamese flak was indeed very heavy, but it was also very concentrated around primary targets such as factories, bridges and road junctions. Once a TAC crew had completed their run in, made the 'pop up' climb and rolled into their attack dive, the time spent 'in the barrel' was mercifully brief. During the bomb run, seconds seemed like hours, but at recommended diving speeds the ground gunners had precious little time to track and fire.

So while the entire F-4 mission in Vietnam was usually conducted at three times the speed of the fastest combats in World War Two and double those of Korea, fundamental things like including a few flak suppressors to divide the gunners' attention and even the odds a little, and mastering a range of high-G evasive manoeuvres and keeping eyes out of the cockpit, rather than down in the 'scopes, for as long and as often as possible, were not really new.

Of course, there was a lot more to it than that. Electronics came to play a bigger part in Vietnam than in any previous war, in that the Phantom's radar, sensors and navigational aids dictated much of what the crew did. In fact electronics controlled a great deal of what the Phantom itself did, and not everyone liked it. So many functions required switching in and switching out that the crew had their hands too full. Fortunately, the degree of automation had not entirely relegated a Phantom crew to the status of passengers, and it was still possible to employ good old manual override, especially if the 'Gee whiz' systems failed to function as advertised.

As Rolling Thunder ground on into its third spring without the USA having very much to show for what was becoming an enormously destructive and costly campaign, the TAC crews in Thailand began wondering how long it was going

A view of the opposition—one of many—taken on a near-suicidal photo run over North Vietnam. All types of target, including airfields, were photographed by Air Force RF-101s and RF-4s, as well as Navy types. These MiG-17s were spotted in revetments at Phuc Yen, 20 miles NW of Hanoi, in the autumn of 1966. (USAF)

to take to subdue North Vietnam by airpower alone. By then, a lot of the most important targets had been attacked many times. These had finally included Vietnamese People's Army Air Force (VPAAF) airfields and other targets that many people felt should have been subjected to a big blitz much earlier, before the defences had been given a chance to multiply. Crews felt that they were somehow paying for their own government's hesitancy and confusion as to how to wage a modern war without actually declaring the fact and thus galvanising the American people to back their military men to the hilt. Laudable though the original efforts to avoid a wider conflict were, they simply did not work.

While similar restrictions, for similar reasons (which also did not work) had been placed on aircrews in Korea, that war had seen something that this one as yet, had not—fighter aces. And, in a comparable period, one hell of a lot of aces, too. Not that the creation of aces was ever the primary F-4 mission, as it had been in Korea with the F-86, but it did help morale to know that the Air Force understood how its fighter pilots felt, and was doing things right as far as the business of air combat went. Thus far, it didn't seem like it at all.

That is not to say that the Phantom crews were failing to rack up MiG kills when they had the chance. By the early spring of 1967 the score had risen to more than 50 MiG-17s and -21s. Somehow, though, something was missing in this war. Perhaps still making comparisons with Korea, and even with Second World War fighter pilots' scores, many felt that the score should have been far greater. On the debit side, MiGs had managed to shoot down but three F-4s in 1966, and only nine were to fall to them in 1967.

Overall, the F-4 losses to MiGs were to amount to 33 for the entire time the type was in combat. On the other hand, this total was equalled in one year (1966) by AAA and small-arms fire, and North Vietnam's ground fire was eventually to account for 307 Phantoms, to which figure must be added the SAM score of 30, again for the whole combat period.

It was true that there were MiGCAP flights on almost every mission, but the job remained paramount in that it was bombs on target by the TAC strike forces that would cause the North Vietnamese finally to capitulate—or so the Pentagon theory ran. Those who had to do the job had realised for a long time that, although the enemy was being hurt by the almost incredible rain of bombs that had been dropped on the North since March 1965, he seemed very reluctant to wave any white flags.

It was therefore left to the Air Force and Navy fighter and fighter-bomber crews to carry on with much the same high risk to life and limb, and to try to ensure that all available aircraft got to the target when a strike was launched, and that they dropped their loads accurately and returned safely. The alternative was a strike force with gaps left by aircraft aborts and combat losses, a reduced weight of explosive on target and fewer aircraft on the line for the inevitable repeat attack.

It had been learned from previous conflicts that to return within hours to the same target area, with a fully alerted defence, was tempting providence. In Vietnam, therefore, the planners tended to wait some time, until the enemy had made temporary repairs, before attempting the same thing again. That kind of policy could lead to a war that dragged on—indeed had already dragged on—for years. While this seemed a strange way to fight a war, it should perhaps be stressed—more than it has been previously—that the Vietnam air war effort was often patchy due to one reason and one reason alone: the weather. For days, sometimes for weeks, the prime targets simply could not be attacked because they were hidden under a dense blanket of cloud or low-lying mist, or often both.

Consequently, to maintain the notorious 'sortie rate', which was run as a kind of inter-service sweepstake by paper-shufflers far removed from the heat of combat, strike forces were sent against a great many alternative targets, sometimes of little or no importance. It was believed that the destruction of minor railroad spurs or small vehicle parks would eventually lead to complete isolation of the main battle front in the South. The fact that there were no friendly troops on North Vietnamese soil to take ground and capture the installations that had been knocked out gave the war an air of unreality. Vietnam was hardly the same as Japan in 1944–45, when airpower achieved a victory without the use of ground forces.

While the Air Force carried out numerous Combat Skyspot blind bombing raids to get around the weather problem, these tended to be far less accurate than sorties where the targets were visible to the naked eye. Electronic detection

More North Vietnamese MiGs under USAF photo interpretation, this time showing one of the rarely-photographed MiG-15UTU two-seat trainers next to the MiG-17 on the left of the picture, which was taken at Phuc Yen. (USAF)

played a large part, but targets 'in the clear' stood more chance of being badly damaged or knocked out, although the latter was rarely possible, even on a good day.

Visual identification of the targets was also necessary in aerial combat. Again, radar played a big part in detecting bogeys, which would usually turn out to be NVNAF MiGs, but on many missions there were numerous friendly aircraft in the air. The F-4 pilots and navigators simply could not take the risk of launching missiles without positive knowledge that they were taking out enemy aircraft, not their own. As in any war, mistakes were made.

By 1967 the USAF wing structure for the war against North Vietnam was well established. There were two F-105 Thunderchief units, the 355th and 388th, based respectively at Takhli and Korat, with the tactical fighter squadrons of the 8th Wing at Ubon. These three wings largely prosecuted the war until the termination of Rolling Thunder in 1968, with a number of squadron rotations within each wing in that timeframe. Strike support was provided by USAF units based in South Vietnam, and there was an equally high commitment by US Navy attack and fighter squadrons flying from the carriers on Yankee Station in the Gulf of Tonkin.

One of three tactical wings then flying F-4Cs from bases in South Vietnam, Col Robert W. Malloy's 366th TFW, regularly flew MiGCAPs into North Vietnam, and had already achieved eight kills. Although they were shouldering the dual combat responsibility of ground support in South Vietnam and the different, though perhaps far more satisfying if more dangerous, war in the North, the 'Gunfighters' won a reputation second to none for hard flying and fighting. Men such as Fred Haeffner, James Hargrove, Samual Bakke and Robert Titus made the 366th a top-notch outfit. Since 14 May the Gunfighters had lived up to their nickname. The wing had become the first in SE Asia to get gun pods for its F-4s, and on that day two MiG-17 pilots had found out the hard way what it was like to fly against a gun-carrying Phantom. A third VPAAF pilot had succumbed to a Sparrow the same day, completing a triple for the 366th.

The 8th Wing was then the premier tactical F-4C unit, tasked only with strike/strike-support missions over the North, and not surprisingly it became the top MiG killing unit of the war. Among its pilots were such notables as Phil Combies, William Kirk, Ed Rasberry, Dick Pascoe—and Robin Olds. Men like Olds, who had been around fighters a long time, tended to be better placed than some of the younger pilots to put the eccentricities of the Vietnam air war into perspective. More importantly, they had the experience (and a little rank, which helped) to cut through the jungle of orders which were at times very much at variance with what they knew to be tactically sound.

When Olds joined the 8th Wing, in September 1966, he set about making some sense of the situation as he found it, and did what he could to minimise losses while still hitting the enemy hard. In January 1967 Operation Bolo, the famous ruse mission, had shown that it could be done—that good old US 'know-how' could fool the usually sharp North Vietnamese and, for once, produce a resounding 7–0 victory.

The spring of 1967 was to bring almost daily contact with the VPAAF, as the F-4s and F-105s pounded enemy targets during a spell of fine weather. Not all rounds of combat manoeuvring with the MiGs brought results. More often than not, if the US MiGCAP could drive off the interceptors sent against the strike force, that was the end of it. The mission was carried out and both sides went home. The enemy did not always stay to fight if his surprise hit-and-run tactics failed. The flak was always there to ensure that the Americans did not have an easy ride.

Conversely, if the sudden, slashing MiG attack caused strike aircraft to jettison their loads to fight on more equal terms, then the weight of bombs on target would be less. Often the MiGs quit at that juncture, their basic defensive task achieved for the day.

On other days, however, the MiGs would be aggressive and definitely stick around to slog it out with the Phantoms and Thunderchiefs. Such a day was 20 May, a date that the participants remember as that of a real dogfight. It mattered little that that term belonged back in the Stone Age of propeller-driven fighters, for a dogfight is what took place.

It started out as just another Rolling Thunder mission—big, brash and expensive, with the usual lavish support that increasingly typified the Air Force effort over the North. Young Tiger KC-135 tankers gave their usual top-notch service to the force on entry into North Vietnam, while an EB-66 provided airborne early warning of SAM and MiG activity. An Iron Hand flight of F-105s was on the lookout for business.

Dual targets had been briefed for the Thuds, the Kinh No motor vehicle repair facility and Bac Le rail yards. Flying as MiGCAP to these respective strikes were two F-4 flights of the Da Nang-based 366th TFW's 389th TFS and two

from the Wolfpack's 433rd Squadron. By routeing the strike force out over the
Gulf of Tonkin, it was over North Vietnamese territory for the minimum
amount of time. Landfall was made at the group of offshore islands, where the
F-4 crews released their centreline drop tanks to prepare for combat.

Target ingress took the US aircraft about 20 miles east of the North
Vietnamese air force base at Kep, located in Route Pack VIB. It was at this point
that two SAMs were fired at the force. The Iron Hand F-105s swung into
action, quickly silencing the batteries with Shrike Anti-Radiation Missiles. When
the ARMs struck home, the SA-2s that had been launched lost their guidance
and presented little further threat to the strike force.

The first MiG warning was called when the force was still 15 miles from the
target area. This disrupted plans to split the F-4 force into two to cover the
separate F-105 bombing runs, as the MiG warnings multiplied. Participating
crews noted the urgency in the strident radio calls, but could have used some
more definite information as to the direction from which the threat was coming,
and how many enemy aircraft had been seen. It was understandable that pilots
wanted everyone to know they were in danger of being attacked, but the correct
R/T procedures were often lacking. It was another problem common to most
air wars.

The MiGs were quickly on the scene, engaging the Phantoms. The Thuds
pressed on to brave the AAA fire, their pilots thankful that at least one element
of the enemy's triple threat temporarily had other things to occupy it. If the F-4
crews could contain the MiGs, they were unlikely to be bothered for the time
being. Up to fourteen MiG-17s manoeuvred with the eight F-4s for the next
fourteen minutes, the North Vietnamese pilots showing unusual spirit for the
contest.

Aircraft Commander Major John Pardo, with 1st Lt Stephen Wayne as his
back-seater, callsign Tampa Three, nailed the first MiG-17 to fall that day.
Seeing four enemy fighters turning in to make a pass on the F-105s (the MiG
drivers were well briefed as to their prime target), Col Olds, orchestrating the air
battle, fired a missile at them, missed, and told Pardo to take care of it. Pardo
complied by attempting to launch one of his Sparrows. The guidance failed, and
he followed up with an AIM-9. This achieved lock-on and homed in on the
number four MiG. One down.

Now there were more MiGs in pursuit of Pardo's aircraft. He abandoned the
attack on the original MiG flight and broke to spoil the aim of this new threat at
his eight o'clock. Observing his MiG kill burning on the ground, Pardo entered
the turning match that had developed, and although he fired more AAMs
during the course of the battle, he could not claim any more positive results.

Lieutenant Colonel Robert Titus and 1st Lt Milan Zimer, callsign Elgin
Three, heard the first MiG warning as they were covering the rear end of the
F-105 force attacking the vehicle works. They were flying down Thud Ridge,
the line of low hills some 20 miles north of Hanoi grimly nicknamed for the
number of F-105s that had gone down in that vicinity. In the lead was the other
366th flight, callsign Buckshot. Titus saw two MiG-21s heading for the Thuds
and, although the MiGs were diving away fast, he 'padlocked' them, meaning he
had picked them up and was going to attack. Elgin Flight lead Bob Janca then
called 'Honeymoon', another code word which told Titus that lead had

The MiG-21 gave North Vietnam increased capability against US aircraft, although some of the top pilots preferred to stay with the tried and trusted MiG-17. In the right hands, the MiG-21 was responsible for a number of US combat losses. (USAF)

acknowledged the action and that he would cover him.

Getting his sight pipper on one of the MiGs, Titus had Zimer go to boresight (visual) and obtained a lock-on. Suddenly, the MiG, which had been rendered highly visible by sunlight reflected from its natural metal surface, disappeared. The F-4 crew switched to radar to reacquire the target. They found it again, but then the lock-on was lost. A turning match ensued, with the MiG rolling and keeping his speed well up. Another lock-on. Phantom and MiG charging away to the northwest, supersonic at 16,000 ft. Then, just as Elgin Three got into missile firing range: 'BREAK!' Titus recognised the voice. 'Three, this is Four. Break hard left!'

Wonderful timing, Titus thought. A MiG square in the sights and back-seater yelling for a missile shot. No way. Extreme folly to ignore the call. Might be a MiG pilot sitting right in our six, finger closing round the trigger. Titus hauled the Phantom round in a full rudder turn.

No attack materialised, so Elgin Three headed back in the direction of the strike force. As Titus pulled their aircraft round in a hard left turn, another MiG-21 was seen. Titus and Zimer were then at 10,000 ft and Mach 1.2, closing on the enemy fighter, having achieved radar lock-on. One missile was fired. Nothing. Titus waited for what seemed an eternity for the Sparrow to drop away and then come up. He heard it zoom away, but it failed to guide. A second AIM-7 did the same thing. Titus, wondering if anything was going to work that day, fired a third Sparrow:

'. . . it tracked beautifully. With a white cloud of smoke behind it, just like an arrow, it started off. We were quite low by now, probably down about six or eight thousand feet above sea level, and yet those mountains were coming up at us. We made a diving turn and I could see this MiG-21 beautifully. There was no doubt about it; red stars on the wing, sun glinting off the fuselage. I told Zimer: 'It's going to hit!', and about that time it hit him right in the left wing root, right next to the fuselage.

There was a tremendous explosion, a ball of orange flame, big black smoke and the wing came off and started tumbling down. The fuselage went, and another object separated from the plane. I remember saying, "He punched out".'

The fact that the enemy pilot managed to eject surprised Titus, who thought he had almost certainly been killed in the fireball. But there he was, swinging under an orange and white 'chute.

In another part of the sky, having better luck with the Sidewinder than Titus had with the Sparrow, was Bob Janca and his back-seater, 1st Lt William Roberts. Spotting a MiG-21 at his 9–10 o'clock-high position, Elgin Lead began a left turn to avoid. The MiG reversed to the right and started to climb, with the F-4 in pursuit. Still going up, Janca obtained a good AIM-9 tone and fired, zero angle-off, with the MiG framed against the blue sky. It was an almost textbook intercept. The missile guided straight and detonated ten to fifteen feet to the right of the MiG's tail. Shedding large pieces, the MiG pitched up and began a roll off to the right from about 8,000 ft. It appeared to Elgin Four to enter a spin before Janca lost sight of it at about 1,000 ft. However, the MiG's demise was seen by Roberts, as well as by the crew of Elgin Two. The victory was confirmed. In return, Janca was able to confirm the Titus/Zimer MiG-17 kill.

Meanwhile, Olds was equally busy. Paired with 1st Lt Stephen B. Croker, he was to add a third and fourth MiG to his score today, to make him the leading MiG killer in South East Asia. Few would have denied the Wolfpack's boss his achievement. Robin Olds stands out as upholding the fine reputation of the American fighter pilot under very difficult conditions. Other very able commanders led the Wolfpack when he completed his tour, but Olds tended to speak out about conditions as he found them, becoming a sort of unofficial/official spokesman for the tactical troops. It is no exaggeration to say that all crews flying missions over North Vietnam gained something from his tenure at Ubon.

Olds described the type of combat that developed on 20 May. From his viewpoint it was:

'. . . quite a remarkable air battle . . . an exact replica of the dogfights in World War Two. Our flights of F-4s piled into the MiGs like a sledgehammer, and for about a minute and a half or two minutes, that was the most vicious, confused dogfight I have ever been in. There were eight F-4Cs, twelve MiG-17s and one flight of F-105s, on their way out from the target, who flashed through the battle area.'

In such a situation there was a triple danger for the American aircraft, not the least of which was that aircraft could easily collide. Olds emphasised this:

'Quite frankly, there was not only danger from the guns of MiGs, but the ever-present danger of a collision to contend with. We went round and round that day with the battles lasting twelve to fourteen minutes, which is a long time.'

A further, though lesser threat, was that a rogue missile might decide that the exhaust of a J79 made a better and nearer target than did the heat of a Tumanskii—or vice versa, as the MiG-21 was itself armed with AAMs, unlike the older MiG-17. A pair of K-13As (AA-2 Atoll), themselves copies of the US AIM-9B, were carried on wing pylons. Otherwise the MiG-21PF and MF variants issued to the VPAAF carried a pod containing a single 23 mm GP-9 cannon on the fuselage centreline.

As the air war developed, so the Americans had noted that the MiG pilots used a number of formations and manoeuvres designed to counter any superior qualities the US fighters might have had. On 10 May, Olds reported:

'This particular day we found that the MiGs went into a defensive circle low down, about 500 to 1,000 ft. In the middle of this circle, there were two or three MiGs circling at about a hundred feet—sort of in figure-eight patterns. The MiGs were in groups of two, three and sometimes four, in a very wide circle.

Each time we went in to engage one of these groups, a group on the opposite side of the circle would go full power, pull across the circle, and be in firing position on our tails almost before we could get into firing position with our missiles. This is very distressing, to say the least.

The first MiG I lined up on was in a gentle left turn, range about 7,000 ft. My pilot achieved a boresight lock-on, went full system, narrow gate, interlocks in. One of the two Sparrows fired in a ripple guided true and exploded near the MiG. My pilot saw the MiG erupt in flames and go down to the left.

We attacked again and again, trying to break up that defensive wheel. Finally, once again, fuel consideration necessitated departure. As I left the area by myself, I saw that lone MiG still circling, and so I ran out about ten miles and said that even if I ran out of fuel, he is going to know he was in a fight.

I got down on the deck, about fifty feet, and headed right for him. I don't think he saw me for quite a while. But when he did, he went mad—twisting, turning, dodging and trying to get away. I kept my speed down so I wouldn't overrun him and I stayed behind him. He headed up a narrow little valley to a low ridge of hills. I knew he was either going to hit that ridge up ahead or pop over the ridge to save himself. The minute he popped over I was going to get him with a Sidewinder.

I fired one AIM-9 which did not track and the MiG pulled up over a ridge, turned left, and gave me a dead astern shot. I obtained a good growl. I fired from about 25 to 50 feet off the grass and he was clear of the ridge by only another 50 to 100 ft when the Sidewinder caught him.

The missile tracked and exploded five to ten feet to the right side of the aft fuselage. The MiG spewed pieces and broke hard left and down from about

200 ft. I overshot and lost sight of him.

I was quite out of fuel (down to 800 lbs, enough for eight minutes flying) and all out of missiles and pretty deep in enemy territory all by myself, so it was high time to leave. We learned quite a bit from this fight. We learned you don't pile into these fellows with eight airplanes all at once. You are only a detriment to yourself.'

The last MiG destroyed in the 20 May air battle went to the lead aircraft of the 8th Wing's Ballot Flight, crewed by Maj Phil Combies and 1st Lt Daniel Lafferty. It was Combies' second victory. Having engaged several MiGs without results, he was climbing to rejoin the battle when he saw a MiG-17 in hot pursuit of a Phantom about $1\frac{1}{2}$ miles away.

Later analysis of the combat showed that this particular F-4 was Olds' machine. Realising that he was being pursued, Olds executed a hard left break. The MiG pilot overshot and headed out towards Kep airfield, some eight miles distant. Combies overhauled him and obtained a good AIM-9 tone. He fired. The missile impacted in the MiG's tailpipe area and caused visible fire. From 1,500 ft the enemy fighter went belly up and flipped over into a dive. Combies and Lafferty saw it hit the ground for a sure victory.

One of those men who attract colourful stories that pass into legend in fighter pilot circles, Combies will long be remembered as one of three crews who carried out the low-level raid on the Thai Nguyen steel works in the Red River Valley on 30 March 1967. Having dropped their bombs and come through that wall of red-hot steel not completely unscathed, Combies and his back-seater went looking for a tanker as they left North Vietnam. Finding one, the F-4 nudged into position, ready to take fuel. The boom operator, intent on his work, suddenly noticed something—the Aircraft Commander of the Phantom was smoking a cigarette! Seeing the boom swing suddenly away, Combies got on the horn to ask why. The boom operator said: 'I can't refuel you sir, until you put out your cigarette'. The story goes that, having taken 20 min to get a smoke going against the slipstream blasting through his shattered windscreen, Combies was not to be denied. There was a pregnant pause. Then came the reply, ice cold: 'Give me the fuel or I'll shoot you down'.

When the Wolfpack and Gunfighter Phantoms landed back at Ubon, there was much elation. It was always good for morale, everyone's morale, to know that the endless man-hours put in to keep each F-4 serviceable under such difficult conditions resulted in combat victories. Enemy aircraft kills had been the primary *raison d'être* for fighter units since the First World War, and even though their Vietnam task had not been thus defined, it did not prevent a feeling of elation. A chance to celebrate was always welcome. The Wolfpack nailed a red star to a board surmounting the entrance to the Ubon flight operations shack every time one of its crews scored, and the events of 20 May brought the total to 21. It appears to have been unrecorded whether the 366th had its own scoreboard, but no self-respecting fighter wing whose daily round included missions over North Vietnam lacked red paint and star-shaped stencils.

It was only through the kind of combat that occurred on 20 May that the Air Force F-4 crews could hone their technique for dealing with the enemy MiG force. While the VPAAF was determined in its task, pilots would rarely stick

Towards the end of the air war over North Vietnam, all the previous years of combat, with strike forces attempting to knock out targets with millions of high-explosive iron bombs on hundreds of thousands of sorties at vast cost in lives and dollars, were rendered obsolete by a small number of high-tech weapons such as the Paveway laser-guided bomb. While it was not infallible, the 'smart' bomb was a hundred times better than conventional ordnance, and impressive results were achieved with it. In this view, a pair of Wolfpack F-4Ds from the 435th and 433rd Squadrons prepare to roll in on the target and release their 750 lb LGBs. (USAF).

around to exploit the basically good qualities of their aircraft, particularly manoeuvrability and heavy cannon armament. Relatively few had had long enough to gain confidence in combat, and there was an understandable reluctance to risk losing aircraft or pilots to superior forces—the learning curve was certainly not restricted to the Americans. Increasingly, the North Vietnamese came to realise that the sheer power of the F-4 could often nullify any advantage the defenders might have held.

An F-4 could nearly always catch a MiG-17, and although the MiG-21 was a more equal adversary in this respect, an alert crew, with the advantage of two pairs of eyes outside the cockpit, could reverse a dangerous situation by exploiting the excellent speed range of the F-4. Apart from fuel considerations, the most serious drawback the Phantoms faced in combat was the low reliability of the missile armament. If the majority of the AAMs fired had found targets, rather than the smaller number that actually did guide correctly, the VPAAF would have sustained much higher casualties. It was the exception to enjoy the kind of 'one-shot' kill such as that achieved by Janca and Robertson on 20 May, the results more usually being similar to those of Titus and Zimer, with the score being the same—one enemy aircraft destroyed—in both cases.

Phantom air-to-air kills, 20 May 1967

Sqn/Wing	Crew	Aircraft	MiG type
389th TFS/ 366th TFW	Maj Robert D. Janca/ 1st Lt William E. Roberts, Jr	64-0748	MiG-21
389th TFS/ 366th TFW	Lt Col Robert E. Titus/ 1st Lt Milan Zimer	64-0777	MiG-21
433rd TFS/ 8th TFW	Maj John R. Pardo/ 1st Lt Stephen A. Wayne	63-7623	MiG-17
433rd RFS/ 8th TFW	Maj Philip P. Combies/ 1st Lt Daniel E. Lafferty	64-0673	MiG-17
433rd TFS/ 8th TFW	Col Robin Olds/ 1st Lt Stephen B. Croker	64-0829	MiG-17
433rd TFS/ 8th TFW	Olds/ Croker	As above	MiG-17

CHAPTER 6

May Day, 1982

The air war over the Falkland Islands during the spring of 1982 was a triumph for British arms in general and the British Aerospace Sea Harrier in particular. Although the actual circumstances were unique, the conflict was not unlike others in some respects. The confrontation with Argentina virtually hinged on the successful deployment of this one aircraft type. It is difficult to imagine how Britain's resolve to remove the enemy from the islands by force could have been achieved, once fighting had broken out, if the Harrier had not been available.

Putting so much responsibility into the hands of pilots flying one good fighter type was in no way new in warfare as conducted by Western nations. In fact, it was fast becoming the normal thing to do. But in the spring of 1982 Britain was in the unenviable position of having to commit not only most of its examples of that fighter, but the majority of the pilots trained to fly it as well. Those factors made the vertical-take-off Sea Harrier's operational debut even more of a calculated risk, for, at the time, there really was very little else available.

Had the Royal Navy not had any carriers at that time, the RAF could conceivably have mobilised the greater part of its own Harrier and Phantom forces, using the base at Wideawake Island, and taken on the Argentinian air strikes, relying heavily on in-flight refuelling en route to the combat area and back. It might have worked. As it was, the flexibility of the Royal Navy carriers, with their ability to put fighters right into the combat area, proved decisive. Not since the Second World War had carriers been obliged to place themselves in harm's way, knowing that the opposing side had an air force and a navy quite disposed to, and almost certainly capable of, sinking these vital assets.

Britain had retained a small carrier force in the face of daunting political opposition. That policy was to pay dividends in the Falklands operation, as the Argentinians suffered a spiralling loss of pilots and aircraft in their efforts to sink British ships and penetrate the 200-mile Total Exclusion Zone thrown around the islands. Argentina's ill-timed gamble was shown up as the costly folly it was, although her leaders could probably be excused for thinking that the Falklands were simply too remote for a military expedition to be sent from a rather larger island nation 12,000 miles away.

At that time, the Royal Navy had in commission two carriers capable of launching fixed-wing air strikes—*Hermes* and *Invincible*. The old *Hermes*, displacing 27,800 tons fully loaded, became the flagship of the task force rapidly assembled to sortie down to the South Atlantic. Able to operate up to 20 aircraft and eight helicopters, *Hermes* was destined to undertake the lion's share of the Sea Harrier sorties during the campaign, her total of embarked aircraft being 50 per cent greater than could be accommodated by the more modern 19,500-ton *Invincible*.

When Argentina made her bid to bring the Falklands within her sphere of influence, she possessed a serviceable strike force of 11 Dassault Mirage IIIs, 46 McDonnell Douglas A-4B/C Skyhawks, 34 Israel Aircraft Industries Daggers and five Dassault Super Etendards, plus 115 Pucara, Aermacchi MB.339 Morane-Saulnier Paris and Beech T-34C Turbo-Mentor light-attack types. There were also six English Electric Canberra B.2s for conventional, medium-altitude bombing.

The Super Etendards had recently had their offensive capability significantly boosted by being modified to use the Aérospatiale AM.39 Exocet air-to-surface missile. Otherwise the force relied on gravity dropped 'iron' bombs from US, British and Israeli sources and, in some cases, from quite ancient stocks, and internal gun armament. In the case of the Mirage, the Matra 530 semi-active radar guided and 550 infrared air to air missiles were also carried.

On paper it was a formidable enough force, shared between the *Fuerza Aerea Argentina* (FAA) and *Comando de Saviacion Naval Argentina* (CANA), and well able to back up operations by the Argentine Army. Combat commitment— and success or failure—would depend on how the aircraft were deployed, the skill of the pilots flying them, and the nature of Britain's response.

That response was Operation Corporate, built around a naval task force assembled in a timescale unprecedented in any equivalent period outside a full national war footing, and a good deal better than any war emergency plan then under consideration. It was spearheaded by the two carriers, each with a complement of Sea Harrier FRS.1s totalling 20 aircraft (800 and 801 Naval Air Squadrons). Both units had been supplemented by aircraft and crews from 899 NAS, and each carrier also had Sea King helicopter units embarked. The carriers and other surface vessels were part of TF 317, the other element being TF 324, the UK submarine force.

Small though their numbers were, Nos 800 and 801 Squadrons were equipped with an aircraft that had for many years been the only combat aircraft in the world capable of vertical/short take-off and landing (VSTOL). It was perhaps surprising that the USSR was the country that followed Britain's enterprising lead in this important field, when the Soviet Navy revealed the Yakovlev Yak-38 Forger as being in service with its first cruiser/carrier *Kiev*, in 1976.

Since the Sea Harrier entered service in May 1981, the Royal Navy had just managed to bridge the gap in fixed-wing capability created by the loss of its last conventional fleet carrier, *Ark Royal*. When the *Ark* went to the breaker's in 1979, there were many who bemoaned the fact, believing it to be almost criminal folly to have no suitable replacement in service or at least on the slipways. It was seen as a dangerous risk to reduce Britain's ability to guard her sea lanes with carrier-borne airpower in the event of war, particularly in the face of growing Soviet naval might.

Some compensation came with the announcement that the service would get the first of a number of 'through-deck cruisers', modestly-sized helicopter carriers. The subsequent decision that these ships should also embark a complement of Sea Harriers—delayed though this was amid almost farcical pontification, groundless ignorant doubts over the aircraft's proven capability, and sheer apathy—was indeed fortuitous. The fact remained that the whole programme was so unbelievably modest in scope—a full squadron of Sea Harriers was established at five (yes, five) aircraft—and so subject to the shrinking national defence purse that it hardly represented much more than a token addition to Britain's defence commitment, which was increasingly being placed in the hands of the RAF and a dubious faith in long-range land-based patrol aircraft.

Thus the 'bargain basement' Navy fixed-wing carrier force just managed to stay in business and the Fleet Air Arm did not become a short-range, all-helicopter force, as was feared when *Ark Royal* was decommissioned. The Falklands campaign was to prove how important that decision was.

The Task Force began sailing from Portsmouth on 5 April 1982. Thousands gathered to cheer the ships on their way, many believing (and not a few hoping) that the breakdown in diplomatic negotiations between Britain and Argentina would not result in war. But as the fleet headed for Ascension Island those hopes showed little sign of being realised; there was no notable Argentinian reaction to the indications that the British meant business. Throughout the Task Force, questions regarding the operational conduct of any conflict on land, at sea or in the air were voiced and mulled over in men's minds. A disturbing factor was that the ships which might be engaged carried no airborne early warning aircraft to detect air attacks. Such aircraft had been pensioned off when *Ark Royal* was scrapped, a move for which the task force was to pay a higher price than might otherwise have been necessary.

If it came to the Sea Harriers having to fly anti-shipping strikes against the Argentine Navy, tactics would have to be devised more or less on the spot, taking due account of the weapons to hand, the degree of opposition and the prevailing conditions. Weather was assumed to play a significant part, as the action would be taking place during the Falklands winter, which invariably brought high winds with extremely low temperatures and poor visibility to that part of the world.

Fortunately, the long voyage provided time to work up the carrier air squadrons to full operational readiness. The scarcity of trained Sea Harrier pilots had meant including in the Corporate roster seven 'fully navalised' RAF pilots and two who had yet to complete their operational flying training. This was largely completed en route, there being an intensive programme of practice interceptions by day and night, air combat manoeuvring and weapons delivery against a variety of different targets using the full range of rockets and bombs carried by the Sea Harrier.

The nearer the task force got to the Falklands, the further out the carriers sent the Sea Harrier CAP, with an increasing number of night sorties. The fighters ranged out to a maximum of 120 miles, and flight operations were even then having to contend with inclement weather which brought mountainous seas and freezing deck surfaces. Very few problems were experienced in operating Sea Harriers, and aircraft serviceability rarely fell below 95 per cent.

At that time, the Sea Harrier FRS.1 was the most modern variant of the series, well equipped for its demanding Naval role. Powered by the Rolls-Royce Pegasus 104 vectored-thrust turbofan offering 21,500 lb of thrust for take off, it had a maximum sea level speed of 740 m.p.h., a transonic dive limit of Mach 1.25, a ceiling of 51,200 ft and a maximum range of 345 miles. Because of budget considerations, the navalised Harrier was specified as a 'minimum-change version' of the RAF's GR.3, and although the aircraft differ considerably, this brief was largely adhered to. For example, the Pegasus Mk.104 was not given any thrust increment for its shipboard role. As well as cost, the ever-present bugbear of weight increase had to be closely monitored. The Sea Harrier did get heavier than the GR.3, but only by 350 lb. The basic operating weights are 12,640 lb for the GR.3 and 12,990 lb for the Sea Harrier. This small difference worked through to a slightly reduced maximum take-off weight, the respective figures being 26,000 lb and 24,600 lb.

Both Harrier and Sea Harrier have inherently good stalling characteristics, which greatly contribute to easy and safe tight turns in combat, particularly at low altitude. Good buffet warning of the onset of a stall enables incidence to be increased, whereupon the aircraft becomes increasingly stable longitudinally. The limit is reached with the stick fully back; the only aerodynamic phenomena are buffet and wing-rock.

Maximum fuel consumption at low altitude is less than one-third that of a typical reheated aircraft, so the Harrier pilot does not have to be deterred from combat manoeuvring for fear of running out of fuel. A further advantage of the Harrier is that the Pegasus is not a heavy smoker, so it does not leave a highly visible exhaust trail.

At the heart of the Sea Harrier's electronic suite is the highly capable Ferranti Blue Fox I-band radar with four main mission operating modes—search; attack with intercept and lead/pursuit or chase for air combat, plus weapons aiming via the head-up display for surface or anti-shipping attack; boresight, for rapid ranging of targets of opportunity; and transponder, for the quick identification of friendly targets.

A feature of RN carrier decks since the early 1980s has been inclined bow ramp or 'ski jump'. Years of VSTOL operation had shown that, with any appreciable load, the Harrier really needed a short, rolling take-off run, just like any other fixed-wing aircraft. If speed of launch took precedence, then VTO was, not surprisingly, the fastest way to go, but on any mission requiring ordnance a roll was preferable. A runway ramp inclined upwards just a few degrees made a world of difference. Theoretical calculation, followed by intensive tests with hardware, proved that lifting a Harrier off a $10°$ incline vastly improved the trajectory of the aircraft. For carrier operation, the ramp launch all but closed the gap between initial acceleration and the aircraft obtaining sufficient flying speed and lift. It also provided a Naval pilot with a vital few extra seconds' flying time 'off the deck', thereby compensating for any loss of power at a critical moment. If the worst happened, the pilot also had a couple of extra seconds in which to initiate ejection.

A $7°$ ski jump was incorporated into the design of *Invincible*, and was an integral part of the deck structure. A 1980 refit bestowed a $7\frac{1}{2}°$ ramp on *Hermes'* deck. This was initially terminated in a flat front section, but before the

A Sea Harrier FRS.1 moments after leaving the ski-jump ramp on the bows of HMS Invincible. *The evident greyness of the South Atlantic was not untypical during the operation to secure the Falkland Islands in the spring of 1982. (British Aerospace)*

Falklands operation it was enclosed by a bulbous 'round down' faired into the port side of the bow.

The boost that this ingenious yet simple modification gave to the Sea Harrier's fairly modest basic weapons load of 5,600 lb (5,000 lb on wing hardpoints, plus 600 lb on a centreline station) can be shown by a couple of examples. A Harrier with a combined fuel/ordnance load of 10,000 lb would need the entire 600 ft to lift off safely from an *Invincible* Class carrier with a level deck. But with a ski jump, a similarly-configured aircraft would need a take-off run of only 200 ft. If full deck length was utilised with a ski jump, the load could be boosted to 13,000 lb.

Weaponry for the Sea Harrier which had not been expended 'in anger' before Corporate was subject to clearances received by the carriers en route. Aboard *Invincible*, 801 Squadron conducted the first live firings of the 2 in rocket, the Lepus flare, and the 1,000 lb air burst (cluster) bomb. Most importantly, the squadron also made the initial live firing of an AIM-9L Sidewinder AAM by a first-line Sea Harrier unit. Designed to hit a target when fired from an aircraft in virtually any attitude, the 'all-aspects' AIM-9L was a vast improvement over previous versions of the Sidewinder, which had required a positive heat-source on which to home, preferably right in front of the launch aircraft.

Vietnam had shown that, while it took an average of two to three shots to hit a target, the Sidewinder was a simple, basically reliable missile, and had often

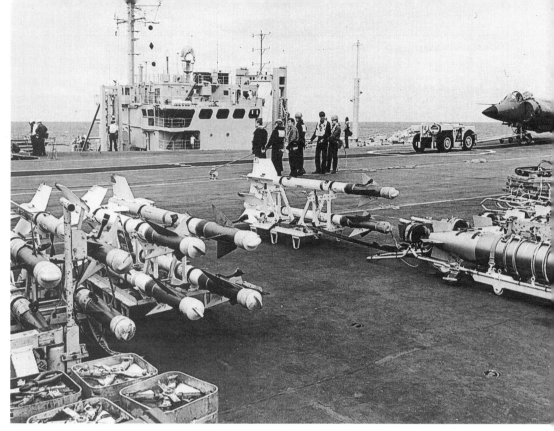

A Royal Fleet Auxiliary alongside one of the Task Force carriers—probably Hermes—*showing racks of AIM-9L Sidewinders and bombs stacked and secured for loading on to the Sea Harriers. US material assistance and support was critical throughout the operation. (British Aerospace)*

A close-up of an AIM-9L under the port wing of a Sea Harrier. The photograph was taken at Yeovilton on the occasion of 800 Squadron's triumphant homecoming from the Falklands. (HMS Heron)

proved better than something more sophisticated. The 'Nine Lima' had a lot of promise, and significantly increased the chance of a sure kill, even if the target aircraft was flying head-on at the aircraft so armed.

While the potent AAMs were considered the primary air-to-air weapon, each Sea Harrier was armed with a pair of 30 mm Aden cannon, each with a tank holding 100 rounds of ammunition as standard or up to 130 rounds if the feed chute space was also filled with shells. Each gun and its ammunition was housed in removable belly packs.

In true British fashion, improvisation was called upon to overcome some deficiencies in equipment. Technicians on 800 Squadron were credited with devising a simple yet effective remedy to the Sea Harrier's lack of active radar countermeasures. Each aircraft had a quantity of chaff, radar-blinding metallised plastic foil, tucked into the ventral rear fuselage air brake recess. Should the passive radar-warning receiver (RWR) indicate that his aircraft was being tracked, the Sea Harrier pilot merely had to deploy his air brakes to release enough chaff to blind the enemy ground or airborne radar that was the source of annoyance.

Intensive flying operations aboard carriers have long necessitated the use of quick and convenient acronyms rather than longer full names or designations to show aircraft and pilot status 'at a glance' at any given time. Thus the Navy had shortened the name of its VSTOL fighter to 'SHAR' to indicate 'on the board' readiness state. This term was also widely used in signals for similar brevity of communication.

As a back-up to any Sea Harriers lost in combat—there were only 28 examples in existence at that time—the RAF was called upon to prepare a force of Harrier GR.3s for movement to the area of forthcoming operations in the South Atlantic. Number 1 Squadron at Wittering responded enthusiastically, despite the fact that their aircraft were primarily used for ground attack. When the possibility of launching their strictly landbound aircraft from carriers was mooted, No. 1's pilots assumed that someone higher up had already thought that one through.

Planning and training for combat was not restricted to the British airmen. Although it possessed one of the strongest air and naval forces in South America, Argentina had, in common with many of her neighbours, been far more preoccupied for years with using elements of the army to quell internal civil unrest—a job that could hardly compare with tackling any kind of trained, well armed military force. Despite decades of veiled and open threats by Argentina that she would one day occupy the Falkland Islands by force of arms, operational deployment plans for taking on an opponent in a full-scale air and/or sea battle had hardly been thought through. In particular, despite the relative modernity of their aircraft, Argentine pilots were not among the world's most experienced, especially regarding the kind of operation the country had brought upon itself. This was more the fault of a chronically over-stretched defence and national budget than any lack of enthusiasm on the part of pilots, but the fact remained that odds of about six-to-one in Argentina's favour against the RN carrier force did not add up to a foregone conclusion as to who would emerge victorious. Many Argentine pilots viewed tangling with Britain with considerable trepidation, notwithstanding homespun propaganda as to the validity of their cause. For one thing, Argentine tactics for attacking ships were almost non-existent. The training to fly low enough to avoid AA fire was definitely lacking, and the speed of the Falklands operation took the bulk of the armed forces by surprise.

Among numerous exacting problems for the defenders was distance. The nearest airfield at Rio Grande is 440 miles from Port Stanley, almost at the limit of the range of the fighters and attack aircraft operated by the Argentinian Air Force. It was assumed that any operations requiring the involvement of Naval strike aircraft would see the country's only aircraft carrier, *25 de Mayo*, in action. The small number of Super Etendards able to launch the Exocet ASM were seen as the most potent part of the Naval force, although the operating unit, the 2nd Escuadrilla, had been in existence only six months, and the pilots had only limited flight time on the aircraft. Even worse was the fact that only a small amount of time had been devoted to calibrating the aircraft's radar and attack computer with the Exocet. When the order to mobilise came, the air force technicians had to go it alone, there being no help from France, which had imposed an arms embargo as soon as the question of ownership of the Malvinas had once again started to figure in Argentinian politics.

The Naval units therefore had the task of persuading their air force colleagues that low flying over the sea to attack ships effectively meant just that—operating altitudes calculated in tens of feet rather than hundreds. To air force pilots, 150 ft was low and 100 ft very low indeed. As subsequent events were to prove, neither was low enough. Although the two-week crash course was demanding for all concerned, the operating height for anti-shipping strikes was reduced.

As Argentine training proceeded and Port Stanley became the terminus for a massive airlift of military supplies, the British Task Force undertook much of its own operational contingency planning for the forthcoming confrontation on the high seas. Few elements had been able to plan for this totally unexpected battle scenario in a location that most of the participants would have been hard put to find on any map, let alone describe in terms of terrain, approach routes, natural obstacles, defensive cover, and so on.

In one respect, the Sea Harrier squadrons had an advantage over all the other would-be combatants. Although they, too, had not had the time to brief themselves on a full range of unexpected contingencies, a pilot rota of combat air patrols for the primary task of protecting the parent carriers was fundamental to shipborne fighters in any navy, anywhere. A CAP would be flown, around the clock if necessary, all the time the carriers were in the combat zone.

As the men of the UK task force used the voyage to the South Atlantic to train and make what battle plans they could, equally feverish activity took place on Ascension Island to prepare for a sizeable influx of British tankers, transports, reconnaissance aircraft, bombers and fighters. The airfield on Ascension, named Wideawake, was about to live up to its name, with more aircraft movements in a single day than had been logged in many months. The first elements of the Task Force arrived at Ascension on 10 April, carrier personnel having busied them-selves during the long voyage with numerous chores, including giving the Sea Harriers coats of low-visibility paint. National markings were dulled down and all squadron emblems obliterated, using sprayguns in the case of *Invincible* and the time-honoured paintbrush in the less-lavishly equipped workshops of *Hermes*.

Sailings from Ascension started on the 18th. Three days later the Argentinians received a positive indentification report from an unlikely surveillance platform, namely a Boeing 707 belonging to Grupo 1 of the Argentine Air Force, that British ships were heading for the Falklands. By that time other elements of the Task Force were in action on South Georgia, so the report should hardly have come as a surprise. The Boeing 707 was in fact the first 'bogey' sighted by an 800 Squadron Sea Harrier on a routine Combat Air Patrol from *Hermes*. On this first encounter the Sea Harrier only photographed the intruder. There was no intention on the part of Britain to be the first to make an aggressive move and perhaps risk escalating a conflict which might, even then, prove to be little more than South American bravado. The Boeing crew, meanwhile, radioed their sighting of British ships and used their cameras to record the Sea Harrier flown by Lt Simon Hargreaves.

By late April Argentinian aircraft had all but completed their migration south to take up residence on their forward operational airfields. They were as ready as they ever would be for a war at short notice. The fighter and attack elements were now located as follows: the Canberra and Learjet reconnaissance force in the hands of Grupo 2 was at Trelew; the Dagger force of Grupo 6 had been split equally, with 17 aircraft each at San Julian and Rio Gallegos, the latter base also temporarily housing the A-4s of Grupos 4 and 5 and the Mirages of Grupo 8; the 2nd Escuadrilla's Super Etendards were already at Rio Grande, and the 3rd Escuadrilla had embarked with eight A-4s in *25 de Mayo*.

On 29 April the carrier, two guided missile destroyers and four smaller destroyers and frigates representing the largest element of Task Force 79, were moving into position to cover the Falklands from the northwest. This force positioned itself just outside the exclusion zone around the islands imposed by Britain on 30 April.

On 1 May Avro Vulcans bombed the airport at Port Stanley as an opening gambit, to show that Britain was serious in her intention to dislodge the Argentine Army from the Falklands. The bomber strike was followed by a two-pronged Sea Harrier attack on enemy installations at Stanley, coinciding with a smaller strike on Goose Green. *Hermes* aircraft undertook the ground-attack sorties, while those from *Invincible* mounted a Combat Air Patrol off the east coast of the islands. It was strongly anticipated that there would be some reaction to these combat sorties, and the Sea Harrier pilots of 801 Squadron were not disappointed, at least in finally seeing enemy aircraft.

The early morning CAP was flown by Fl Lt Paul Barton and Lt Cdr John Eyton-Jones, each flying Sidewinder-equipped aircraft. The first radar contact put two bandits at 120 miles, closing rapidly from the west, followed by two more, and then another two. Lacking an accurate altitude fix, the British pilots searched in vain for what was assumed to be a low-level attack. The enemy was finally located, in the form of six Mirages, at 35,000 ft.

Quite apart from the prime operational consideration of protecting ships from low-level attack, the Sea Harrier pilots on CAP duty had no intention of 'mixing it' with higher-performance enemy fighters at that altitude. For their part, the Argentinians would have preferred the Harriers to come up to them. Both sides naturally wanted to fight at the altitude that best suited their aircraft.

This first contact was inconclusive, as neither side would be drawn. The

The lighter colour scheme of aircraft embarked in HMS Invincible *is evident in this view of a Sea Harrier of 801 Squadron, displaying one Mirage kill stencil under the cockpit. (HMS Heron)*

Argentinian pilots appeared to have considerable hesitation in manoeuvring with the nimble Harrier and its modern weaponry—and they subsequently admitted that this was so. Armed with old examples of the Matra 550 Magic infrared homing and Matra 530 AAMs, plus a pair of 30 mm cannon—weapons which were, on the face of it, more than adequate—the FAA pilots nevertheless wanted more time to evaluate the situation. They had all but run out of that, for their fuel gauges had now indicated that it would be prudent to break off and return home.

It was midday before the next air confrontation took place. Again inconclusive, it did enable the British to prevent a strike by T-34C Turbo-Mentors based at Port Stanley interfering with RN ships preparing to bombard their airfield. Flying the afternoon Sea Harrier CAP were Lt Cdr Nigel 'Sharkey' Ward and Lt Mike 'Soapy' Watson of 801 Squadron. Three Mentors from the 4th Naval Attack Escuadrilla spotted the British aircraft at about the same time they themselves were seen. Opening up with cannon fire, Ward saw no results as the enemy machines sought cloud cover. When the T-34s reappeared they were seen to jettison their bombs and head back to Port Stanley.

Back on their patrol line, Ward and Watson then came across two Mirages, flying fast and obviously under ground control. Once again, apart from the

Argentinian pilots firing off at least three missiles in the optimistic hope that a Sea Harrier might run into them, there was no result. It was not until late afternoon that the CAP found more trade.

This time the Argentinian attack was against ships, and consisted of about 40 sorties flown by Canberras of Grupo 2, A-4s of Grupos 4 and 5, and Daggers of Grupo 6, covered by Grupo 8's Mirages. Paul Barton was also on the CAP that intercepted this strike, with Lt Steve Thomas as his wingman. The British pilots, flying at 11,000 ft, were vectored on to a pair of Mirages by their control ship, *HMS Glamorgan*. The enemy fighters were spotted flying in echelon formation—hardly the best in the circumstances. Both Sea Harriers were in defensive battle formation, flying line abreast with about one mile lateral separation. Thomas took over as lead while Barton veered off, opening out the formation a little more. The Grupo 8 pilots held their unwieldy formation. Mirages and Sea Harriers were closing fast. Thomas was flying at 400 kt indicated airspeed, while Barton was even faster at 550 kt and was pulling around to the right to try coming in on the Mirages' six o'clock position.

Still the Mirages held their formation, and the British pilots felt they could catch them in a pincer, by positioning one aircraft on each flank. The Argentine pair came on. It occurred to the RN pilots that these two were merely bait, with further Mirages watching the proceedings from high above, waiting their chance to pounce. This did not appear to be the case, however, as no other aircraft were seen or picked up on radar.

Both Sea Harriers were rapidly getting into an ideal position for a pincer attack. Barton would be the 'shooter', opening fire from behind. He acquired the Argentinian No. 2 on radar and got a positive lock-on. He had less success with Sidewinder lock-on. There was no tone, so it was pointless to launch. As the Mirage passed within gun range Barton fired off a few rounds of 30 mm while he was still in the turn. He hardly expected a lucky hit, and there was no evidence of the shells having hit the enemy fighter. As the No. 2 Mirage passed across the nose of his aircraft, Barton observed no evasive action, nor anything to suggest that his presence, let alone his gunfire, had even been noticed.

Both Mirages were now coming into the missile envelope of Thomas' Sea Harrier, who picked them up visually at around eight miles. Again no AAM lock-on was possible, and Thomas then saw the lead Argentinian launch a missile from a head-on position, some five miles distant. He watched the missile career off to his left and dive into the sea. He also noticed something fall from one of the Mirages, and assumed this to be an AAM that had failed to pick up guidance. The Mirages passed under the Harrier, which began a hard right turn. There was less than 100 ft separation between the opposing fighters as the Argentinians carried on in trail formation, making a shallow turn to port with the No. 2 about a quarter of a mile behind the leader.

Giving chase, certain that neither he or Thomas had yet been seen, Barton got a good Sidewinder tone on the No. 2 Mirage at 12,000 ft altitude and was well set up in the Argentinian's six. He fired his port side AAM at the aircraft, which was flown by Lt Carlos Perona, and thought at first it had failed to pick up guidance. Unfamiliar with the Sidewinder (this being the first time he had ever fired one), Barton lost sight of the missile as it dropped away from its wing rack to find its trajectory. A very long four seconds passed before Barton saw the Nine Lima streaking into the target.

Perona realised he was under attack only when his aircraft began to break up in the fireball created by the missile strike. Seeing this, the British pilot assumed that the Argentinian had not had time to get out. Perona could have confirmed that a tumbling, burning Mirage makes a less than perfect platform for an ejection, but he survived the bale-out to walk ashore on West Falkland.

It transpired that the Harriers had been seen as the two pairs of fighters crossed over, and Perona thought he might have collided with one of them. This led to Argentine press reports that a Sea Harrier had been destroyed during this action.

On the tail of the lead Mirage, Steve Thomas confirmed that the Harriers appeared to have finally been seen but that the Mirage pilots appeared uncertain as to what action they should take. The leader now made a hard left diving turn, and Thomas was above him. He rolled into a vertical descent, obtained missile lock-on, and fired, just as this aircraft, flown by Capt Garcia Cuerva, entered cloud.

Unseen by Thomas, the Nine Lima's proximity fuse had detonated very near the Mirage and damaged it badly. With his fuel tanks punctured, Cuerva decided to head for Port Stanley rather than risk a run for home base. Unfortunately the gun crews tasked with the defence of Port Stanley had neglected their aircraft recognition training. Cuerva eased his crippled Mirage in from the western end of the airfield and jettisoned his drop tanks for a safer landing. All hell broke loose. The Argentinian gunners, thinking the approaching aircraft had dropped bombs, ranged in and hit it twice. The Mirage went in, killing Cuerva.

While the Mirages were taking attrition higher up, the Argentinian main element was boring in low on the Task Force. Three Daggers of Grupo 6 made a bombing and strafing run on *Glamorgan*, *Arrow* and *Alacrity*, but none of the vessels was badly damaged. Their fuel low, the Daggers dashed for home.

Number 800 Squadron had a CAP up at this time, and Flt Lt Tony Penfold and Lt Martin Hale made contact with more Grupo 6 Daggers. The Argentinian fighters opened this engagement by firing a Shafir AAM, which chose Hale's Sea Harrier as its target. The Daggers had been seen at 12 o'clock when the Harriers were at 20,000 ft. The enemy fighters were at 30–35,000 ft, and the Shafir appeared as a contrail, coming down and turning. Hale broke to port, dumped chaff, and went into a vertical dive. The missile followed.

As he entered cloud at 5,000 ft, Hale looked back to see the missile waver then fall away, obviously with its lock-on broken. Hale reasoned that it had been fired from too great a range, and thankfully turned back into the fray. As he climbed, he heard Penfold call in a missile launch. He looked up and saw a high missile trail, then an explosion. Lieutenant José Ardiles' Dagger, the one that had launched the Shafir, had blown up. The second Dagger broke off the combat and returned to base.

In the gathering dusk six Grupo 2 Canberras from Trelaw bored in, in two flights of three. Picked up by seaborne radar, they were reported to Lt Cdr Mike Broadwater and Lt Al Curtiss of 801 Squadron. Making a radar search at 5,000 ft, both Sea Harriers made contact. Dropping down, Curtiss pulled a

A machine of 800 Squadron shows the darker Sea Grey colour scheme and two kills, a Mirage and a Skyhawk, displayed. (HMS Heron)

pursuit curve and launched a Sidewinder at a Canberra flying some 50 ft above the sea, about 150 miles out of Port Stanley. It hit the No. 2 aircraft in the flight, piloted by Lt de Ibanez. As the bomber continued to fly with one engine on fire, Curtiss lined up for another shot. He had seen the first AAM explode close to the aircraft and observed debris fall from it without it apparently suffering conclusive damage. His second AIM-9 was still in flight as the Canberra ditched, both pilot and navigator having ejected. No trace of either crewman was found.

Seeing Broadwater closing in, the Canberra flight leader screamed for a break. He turned right and the No. 3 aircraft went left. Broadwater fired both his Sidewinders at one of the enemy bombers, but was then forced to break off, low on fuel, and return to *Invincible*. Neither Sidewinder hit the Canberras.

As nightfall on 1 May brought a lull in activity, there was time for both sides to reflect on the first full day of action. For the Sea Harrier pilots there was much elation, tinged with the certainty that British casualties were inevitable if the Argentinians continued to fight in a similar manner. While the enemy pilots clearly had little idea of modern air combat tactics, their propensity to launch missiles, even from ranges that were far too great, gave rise to concern. Sooner or later, it was felt, even a rogue missile would find a target. From the Argentinian point of view there was some merit in these odd tactics, although there is little doubt that they were anything more than hasty reaction to the situation as it arose. A Sea Harrier, forced to out-distance an AAM, burned up fuel and was very likely be forced out of the immediate battle area. Providing the missile did not hit, when it finally gave up the chase the pilot might well have difficulty in finding the enemy formation again. Equally, with a low fuel state, he would have little choice but to return to his carrier. Any such action would have reduced the odds in the Argentinians' favour, although it would have taken a fairly vivid imagination for any Dagger or Mirage pilot to have reported that he was actually outnumbered by the British aircraft.

Vague as it sounds, the foregoing probably implies more of a tactical plan than the Argentinians had. As the reports of the 1 May combats show, the Argentinian pilots were hardly ultra-alert to the presence of British aircraft, and their fighter tactics could have been improved simply by reading a couple of pilot accounts of combat in World War Two. Even decent novels of that period would have emphasised the fact that you do not, in any circumstance, try to penetrate defended airspace without your high cover, and that to fail to initiate any form of mutual defence by basic eyeball observation is a recipe for disaster. The actions of the Mirage pilots indicated that they were placing far too much faith in their radars to tell them where the enemy was—another highly dubious practice, and all but useless without the back-up of eyes looking outside the cockpit.

At the outset of the Falklands campaign there was some doubt as to how the Harrier would perform in actual combat. This factor, despite being the one that all military pilots have trained for ever since the aeroplane was shown to have a military purpose, has remained in doubt for years with some types. In more than a few cases, a given type never has had the chance to prove that it performs as its designers predict.

It was said somewhat disparagingly that the Harrier was a subsonic fighter in a supersonic age, was far too small to carry a decent load, and was too short-ranged. Such people admitted that it was a very good airshow performer—often, in fact, the one aircraft that the general public came to see at such events—due mainly to its unique 'up, down and backwards' flight character-istics. Before the South Atlantic became a battleground, Harrier pilots had few counters to any doubts that the modestly-dimensioned VSTOL fighter could do as well as other types, nearly all of which dwarfed the marvel from Kingston, not only in overall dimensions but in load-carrying capability. In the final analysis, only combat could provide the necessary proof, one way or the other.

That the Sea Harrier did so well was to the credit of both the aircraft itself and Royal Navy training. The pilots in action in the South Atlantic did not indulge in any fancy flying techniques stemming from the unique capabilities of their aircraft. Some of the manoeuvres the Harrier can perform had been proved to have no real material advantage in combat. Pilot experience on type counted for a great deal, despite the fact that the navalised Harrier was not available in great numbers. That, and the availability of the AIM-9L Sidewinder, made the difference.

On the Argentinian side, the fairly modest losses on the first day of the aerial conflict had very far-reaching effects. The South Americans had lost two Mirages, one Dagger and a Canberra. The shoot-down by friendly flak over Port Stanley was not then known, but reports had been received that the gunners had despatched a number of British aircraft. The fact remained that

The cockpit of the Sea Harrier FRS.1, showing salient details. A HUD surmounts the central vertical panel, with the main flight instruments below it. The white spot on the right is the radar warning receiver, below the Blue Fox radar scope, mounted at top right of the instrument panel, itself covered by a detachable cover. In this view the ejector seat has also been removed. (British Aerospace)

four aircraft had not returned to base.

As they had suspected, the Argentinians had nothing to match the AIM-9Ls carried by the Sea Harriers. This fact alone brought dismal realisation that forcing the British fleet to withdraw from the Falklands would be a near-impossible task while the ships had air defence of such calibre. This fact was really taken to heart by the Argentinians, who subsequently avoided air combat with the British CAP, which they nicknamed 'the Black Death', for 20 days, until the task force put its invasion forces ashore from the beach-head in San Carlos Water on the 21st, Argentine Navy Day.

Another sobering thought to concentrate Argentine minds was the bombing of Port Stanley by the RAF Vulcans. They reasoned that, if the war became too costly through air attacks on the fleet, there was little doubt that the British could and would bomb Argentinian airfields. Therefore, it was deemed prudent to remove the Mirage force from combat operations over the Falklands and pull them back to defend friendly airspace in that eventuality.

Thus Argentina all but abandoned any hope of gaining air superiority over the Falklands. By withdrawing the one aircraft that could have made the difference, they effectively left their colleagues in the less capable Daggers and Skyhawks an extremely hazardous task in attempting to sink British ships.

That said, in the coming weeks individual pilots would acquit themselves remarkably well, and indeed take a fearful toll in British lives and ships. But without air superiority, the Argentine forces were doomed to a gruelling war of attrition. It did not take much imagination to judge that they themselves would run out of aircraft before the British ran out of ships, or that the UK Government might send in reinforcements once the will to secure the islands had been demonstrated. Once British troops had landed in Port Stanley, dislodging them was a task that was all but beyond the capability of the conscript troops employed. Although these men were well equipped with modern weapons, and could eventually have made themselves far more difficult to dislodge if there had been time to prepare good defensive positions, the speed of the actions mitigated against them. With the Brits established ashore, an Argentinian with a sense of history might well have had cause ruefully to recall a succinct and apt phrase from World War Two—'Enemy on island: issue in doubt'.

When the Falkland Islands were restored to their former peaceful state, the results of the air and sea action were added up. Argentina's challenge to Britain had cost her dearly, but the conflict was far from being one-sided, and her attack pilots had fought a particularly difficult and courageous campaign against qualitatively, if not numerically, heavy odds. Those odds were primarily stacked against her by the magnificent performance of the Sea Harrier, which was responsible for all of the air-to-air kills.

The tally was impressive: 23 Argentinian aircraft destroyed for the loss of six Sea Harriers, none of which was due to aerial combat. Ground fire claimed two, and four were lost to operational causes. A further three Harrier GR.3s were lost by the RAF.

The bulk of the Argentinian losses were suffered by the Mirage/Dagger force, 11 being shot down by AIM-9L AAMs. Six Skyhawks also succumbed to the Nine Lima, as did a Canberra. A C-130 Hercules was despatched by a combination of missile and 30 mm cannon fire, and two Skyhawks and one Pucara were shot down by gunfire alone. Sea Harriers and Harrier GR.3s destroyed a further nine aircraft on the ground, using a combination of cannon fire and cluster bombs.

To achieve this scoreboard the RN deployed a total of just 28 Sea Harriers, and the RAF ten GR.3s. The bulk of the fighting was done by the original Sea Harrier complement aboard the carriers, which totalled 20 aircraft. It would be difficult, if not impossible, to find any comparable air combat achievement that came anywhere near Operation Corporate for sheer tenacity in the face of daunting conditions, both man-made and natural, especially one starting with such an amazingly small number of aircraft.

During its period of combat, the Sea Harrier flew more than 1,100 CAP sorties and 90 offensive support missions. To these were added 2,000-plus south of Ascension Island and another 1,650 within the TEZ. These figures

The magnificent performance put up by Sea Harriers against Argentine air forces in the South Atlantic served to show that good aircraft, well trained pilots and sound tactics can pay off, even if the enemy has numerical superiority. Apart from the addition of the missing Sidewinder, the Task Force CAPs were flown by aircraft in the configuration shown. (HMS Heron)

represented up to ten sorties per day for every aircraft during the combat phase, or up to four sorties for each pilot. There was an average availability of 1.2 pilots per aircraft in the initial stages of the conflict, this subsequently rising to 1.4.

The extremely high aircraft availability rate, established from the earliest days of the task force embarkation, never dropped below 95 per cent. This figure, returned by 800 Squadron in *Hermes* and even improved upon by 801 in *Invincible*, which had a better than 99 per cent availability for all 600 or so operational missions tasked during the conflict, surprised even the British Aerospace industry team aboard the carriers to keep an eye on their charges and advise the squadron technicians should any problem arise. The record proves that they may have found themselves with little to do!

In total, the Sea Harriers flew 2,376 combat missions, representing 2,675.8 hr. It is hard to imagine how such a staggering record of achievement could have been bettered. Perhaps no better accolade is needed than to repeat the words of Admiral Sir Henry Leach, RN, the First Sea Lord and Chief of Naval Staff, who said: 'Without the Sea Harrier there could have been no Task Force'.

In summing up the Harrier's combat debut, nobody should form the impression that the Argentinians were considered a walkover. Most combats took place at low altitude (between 50 and 500 ft), at speeds of around 550 kt IAS. Most involved high load factors demanded by manoeuvres in an essentially horizontal plane. It was certainly true that the Sea Harrier, with a thrust-to-weight ratio of around 1:1, fought at its ideal height, but this and other factors were dictated by the nature of the Argentinian attacks and the kind of targets they were tasked to hit. There was certainly no shortage of courage in the cockpits of the A-4s and Daggers. As one pilot said at the time: 'They were all Fangios'.

On the British side, the only sad note for the entire Sea Harrier force was the loss of four pilots: Lt Cdr John Eyton-Jones (801 Sqn), Lt Alan Curtiss (801 Sqn), Lt Nick Taylor (800 Sqn), and Lt Cdr Gordon Batt (800 Sqn). Taylor was killed on 4 May during a ground attack on Goose Green. His aircraft was hit, probably by 35 mm Oerlikon fire. Some doubt remains as to the circumstances surrounding the loss of Eyton-Jones and Curtiss, both of whom failed to return from a CAP on 6 May. The weather was appalling, and it could only be assumed that the aircraft collided in cloud. Lt Cdr Batt's aircraft crashed in stormy seas just after a night take-off from *Hermes* on 24 May.

The pilots of the other two Sea Harriers lost during Corporate were rescued, these being Lt Cdr Mike Broadwater (801 Sqn), whose machine slid off the deck of *Invincible* while it was taxi-ing forward to take off on 24 May, and F/Lt Ian Mortimer, RAF (attached to 801 Sqn), who was picked up after a nine-hour search-and-rescue mission to locate his dinghy following the destruction of his aircraft by a Roland SAM on 1 June.

When the ceasefire was signed by the Argentinians on 14 June the Falkland Islanders could look forward to a period of relative calm for the foreseeable future, although many of the inhabitants of those remote, barren tracts of land in the middle of the South Atlantic Ocean knew things would never be quite the same again.

Relief that the Argentinians had finally shown the hand they had threatened to play for decades was tinged with the slight apprehension that they might conceivably try again, although there was far less likelihood of that after the 1982 conflict. Like it or not, the Falklands were now very much on the map.

Britain laid long-term plans to consolidate the military victory she had won by bringing limited development to the islands in various ways, not the least of which was to open Port Stanley to civil air traffic. Today, a decade after the war, a British military presence also remains, as it undoubtedly will in some form for some time to come.

CHAPTER 7

Storm over Iraq

Author's note:
In including a final chapter on the Gulf War in this record of fighter combat in different wars, the writer has opted to finish with RAF Tornado ground-attack operations, rather than air-to-air combat. There was, in any event, a notable lack of Iraqi fighter interception by the Tornado F.3s sent to the area, all such success in this respect going to other air forces. It was nevertheless felt that the valuable contribution of the GR.1/1A composite squadrons in the air-land-sea battle was worthy of inclusion, as it illustrates how, in modern warfare, the spearhead has tended to pass from the dedicated fighter and bomber to the strike aircraft.

At 01:00 hr local time (00:12 GMT) on the night of 16/17 January 1991, 12 Royal Air Force pilots opened the throttles of their Panavia Tornadoes and screamed off the runways at Bahrain and Dhahran in Saudi Arabia. Training was over, and Operation Desert Storm was on. Each aircraft had previously had its air data computer programmed with the co-ordinates for Tallil airfield in south-eastern Iraq, one of the main air bases supporting the regime of Saddam Hussein. Flying in the chill pitch dark of the desert night, the RAF force comprised four Tornado GR.1s from Dhahran and eight from Bahrain.

At 30 tonnes take-off weight each Tornado was heavy, carrying two of the massive JP 233 runway denial munitions under the fuselage and a pair of 495 gal fuel tanks, plus a BOZ-107 chaff/flare dispenser and Sky Shadow jammer on the outboard wing pylons. A pound or two of weight was inevitably taken up by a coat of 'desert pink' paint, local camouflage applied to all RAF combat aircraft in the theatre to cover their standard green-grey European colour scheme.

En route on that first mission the crews were comforted by the thought that, whatever reaction Iraq may make to their incursion, they had massive support from Allied airpower. Wild Weasel F-4G Phantoms from the USAF's 35th TFW had gone in ahead of the British aircraft, using their electronics and weapons to confuse, blind and destroy enemy gun and missile radars. To keep the Iraqis guessing as to the location and direction of the strike forces, Lockheed F-117 Stealth fighters had already left their high-explosive calling cards on targets in Baghdad. These were the communications centres, whose primary task was to

A section of Tornado GR 1s over typical featureless Gulf terrain, with ZD809/BA, 'Awesome Annie', nearest the camera. Each aircraft carries a pair of the huge JP 233 airfield denial munitions pods under the fuselage, plus drop tanks, chaff, and ECM pods on all four wing stations. (14 Squadron, via British Aerospace)

direct the gun and missile defences.

The opening of Desert Storm coincided with highly unseasonal bad weather, a factor that was, as in most previous wars, to have a bearing on the conduct of air operations. Modern weaponry still relies heavily on clear conditions for the best possible results, and, as the Allied air offensive opened, heavy fog and cloud would be among the negative factors to be contended with. On the other hand, JP 233 delivery was best accomplished in darkness or overcast conditions, the

The Tornadoes' terrain following radar was not overtaxed during the Gulf War, but aircrews under fire ran the risk of flying into the ground if forward pressure on the stick was just that bit too much. In this view a pair of GR 1s survey the landscape, with ZA470/FL nearest. (14 Squadron, via BAe)

very-low-level target run carrying considerable crew risk if the attacking aircraft could be accurately tracked on ground defence radar.

On the night of 16/17 January the weather did not hamper the Tornado crews, whose arrival over Tallil achieved complete surprise. It was not that the Iraqi gunners were asleep, but they appeared to have no method of predicting the incoming RAF aircraft. They tended to fire up into the sky when their targets were low—very low.

Each Tornado crew released the deadly bomblets and antipersonnel mines over the runways and taxiways, then streaked for their home bases, everyone breathing a sigh of relief that there had been no personnel injuries and no aircraft losses in this most dangerous form of ground attack. Even as the first wave of Tornadoes taxied in, the second strike of the night was ready to go, the crews wondering perhaps if it was they who would be the main target for the now-alerted defences, which the initial attackers had been lucky to evade.

In the UK and USA the first news many people had that US President George Bush had finally ordered the liberation of Kuwait by military force came in the early hours of the 17th, via the television screen. After weeks of media speculation on the possible outcome of the war, suddenly, a few minutes after midnight GMT on Thursday, it was the real thing. Around the Saudi bases, correspondents and film crews confirmed that the first air strikes had indeed gone in, and in Baghdad a CNN TV team put out the first pictures of barrage AAA fire over the city. That particular US television team was to become world famous within a matter of hours.

As the first strikes and Combat Air Patrols were flown, Allied aircrews continued to witness an incredible display of pyrotechnics in the night sky over Iraq as multiple guns pumped shells straight up into the sky as fast as their sweating crews could load and fire. That this was little more than a morale booster for the Iraqi populace, the majority of whom were convinced that their leader had gone too far this time, was only realised later, when it was known how seriously the early raids of 17 January had disrupted the defence network. The fire was wild and undirected, the gunners hoping merely for a lucky hit.

The scream of jet engines, the whistle of falling bombs and the dull crump of explosions made many of Saddam Hussein's subjects fearful that the 'liberation' of Kuwait by their own army the previous August might have been a terrible mistake after all. The belief widely publicised in Iraq, that the United Nations coalition was a mere paper tiger, was proving to be disinformation at its worst.

The men tasked with making that apprehension a reality went to war with the very latest equipment in the Allied inventory. In the air, on land and at sea, the mighty 28-nation coalition force was qualitatively (if not numerically) all but invincible if the war stayed conventional and if its carefully planned battle tactics worked. Preparations for combat operations were overlaid with the sobering knowledge that Iraq possessed a stockpile of chemical and possibly biological weapons, and more than enough missile capability with which to deliver them. In some quarters it was believed to be only a matter of time before initiation of the first overt use of such agents in a major conflict since World War Two.

Despite the sophistication of Allied weapons and equipment, much of it widely tested under simulated combat conditions—not to mention previous 'hot' wars—Iraq's barren desert terrain presented even the best and most sensitive electronic surveillance equipment with an immense challenge. Saddam Hussein was known to have an army numbering at least 590,000 men, including the fanatically-loyal Republican Guard, supported by 4,200 tanks, 3,000 artillery pieces and 500-plus surface-to-surface missiles, deployed south of Basra. These massive forces were backed up by 500 combat aircraft and 250 helicopters, according to the latest Allied estimates.

Saddam's ground units, particularly his missile launchers, were widely dispersed and hidden in a network of concrete underground bunkers dotted around Iraqi territory, which covers an area of approximately 167,000 square miles, a land mass larger than the US State of California. The country has three distinct geographical regions—the central fertile valleys which follow the courses of the Tigris and Euphrates rivers, a mountainous northern area, and the arid steppe desert west of the Euphrates. It was in this latter region that the major military bases were located.

The Tigris and Euphrates were spanned by many bridges which, if an extensive ground war ensued, would be vital targets and were labelled 'Saddam's nerve ends' by Allied Supreme Commander Gen Norman Schwartz-kopf. Basra, the second city of Iraq after Baghdad, is located at the junction of the two rivers, and was known to be a vital link in the enemy communications network since Saddam Hussein's rise to power.

After the August 1990 Iraqi takeover, Kuwait City had itself been strongly fortified by occupying troops. Extensive land minefields had been laid, and a mine belt also protected coastal waters off Kuwait between Bubiyan Island and the capital. This ruled out the possibility of an amphibious landing early in the Allied campaign to retake Kuwait under the terms of UN Security Council Resolution 678.

Against Saddam's military might, the Allies could count on 1,800 US combat aircraft, both land- and carrier-based, plus 435 aircraft from Allied nations, 135 of which were deployed by the RAF on the eve of the outbreak of hostilities. During the course of the campaign, Allied aircraft numbers increased, reaching 2,790 by the time the land battle opened.

If Iraq chose to offer a spirited challenge to the Allies, the war had every likelihood of being both bloody and protracted. Disaster scenarios came thick and fast—in fact there were very few projections that had a positive 'short victory' outcome, because most observers firmly believed that the Iraqi dictator would simply fight to the last man to hang on to Kuwait, his so-called '19th province of Iraq'.

It was therefore decided that airpower would be unleashed against Iraq to more or less swamp the defences, destroy or render untenable all known airbases and military complexes, and establish air superiority over the Iraqi Air Force as quickly as possible. Although seasoned military personnel know full well that projected battle plans can go alarmingly awry in a real war because the opposition can react entirely unpredictably, control of the air had long since been a paramount requirement. Even before the shooting started, Saddam Hussein's lack of reaction to the build-up had challenged established war scenarios. The Allied coalition was given a full six months to position aircraft, armour and ships, so that, by the time the ultimate United Nations deadline for Iraq to pull out of Kuwait came round, the kingdom was ringed with firepower.

Britain's military contribution to the Gulf crisis—Operation Granby—began as early as August 1990, when Bahrain (Muharraq) received the first dozen Tornado GR.1s from Bruggen. RAF Germany would eventually supply all the Tornadoes used in the Gulf War, although the aircraft were flown by mixed crews from both UK- and German-based squadrons, all of which were composite in nature for the duration of operations.

For the RAF, the Tornado commitment was proportionally high. From a

Most of the necessary controls in the front cockpit of the Tornado GR.1 are shown in this manufacturer's fish-eye-lens photograph. The demanding task of monitoring the instruments, keeping the aircraft straight and level at a few hundred feet at night, while people on the ground tried to shoot you down, can easily be appreciated. (BAe)

A Tornado F.3 ground crew working under a shelter that gives at least partial shade at sun-baked Dhahran. Owing to the almost total air superiority achieved by the Allies early in Desert Storm, the RAF fighters had virtually no contact with the Iraqi Air Force. (Crown copyright)

total of 84 aircraft allocated for Gulf operations (and receiving desert paint-work), 67 were actually positioned in the theatre and 61 were operational. The number allocated was a little over half the force of GR.1s, around 110, deployed by the eight RAF Germany squadrons, this in turn being approximately half the total number of aircraft delivered to the RAF. The second squadron, composed of Laarbruch aircraft but flown mainly by crews from Marham, arrived at Bahrain starting 19 December, these machines and personnel moving to Tabuk in Saudi Arabia from 8 October. The six GR.1A reconnaissance aircraft were also from Laarbruch, and these were stationed at Dhahran by 16 January.

Number 15 was the lead squadron at Muharraq, although the 15 aircraft on strength were flown by crews from Nos. IX, 17, 27, 31 and 617 Squadrons. As Tabuk's lead squadron, No. 16 was similarly composed of a mixed complement of crews drawn from the front-line Tornado force—2, IX, 14 and 20 squadrons, with additional representation by Nos. 13 and 617 after the war began. Tabuk also had 15 aircraft, as had Dhahran, where No. 31 was the lead squadron with crews from 9, 14 and 17 squadrons as well as Nos. 2 and 13, which supplied reconnaissance crews for the GR.1As.

Depending on their role, most Tornadoes used in combat had what came to be known as Gulf War or Operation Granby updates and modifications; all examples were powered by the uprated Rolls-Royce RB.199 Mk. 103 turbofan with reheat. Previously unproven in action, the entire Tornado weapons system was carefully monitored to see how it performed under the rigours of combat in a hostile natural environment. The war also served not only to speed up the delivery of the new British Aerospace Alarm anti-radiation missile, which as late as January had hardly been test-fired, but almost to exhaust existing stocks and available production capacity, once its outstanding operational value had been demonstrated.

The RAF strike force enjoyed immense support from coalition nations, particularly the United States, which provided direct combat support and a round-the-clock AWACS radar watch on Iraq for the benefit of all participating aircrews. As the largest air base in Saudi Arabia, Dhahran soon broke all previous records for military aircraft movements, the Tornado GR.1 contingent co-locating with 18 Tornado F.3s and no fewer than 96 USAF F-15C/D Eagles. Tabuk also housed 29 F-15s and 20 BAe Hawks of the Royal Saudi Air Force, while Nimrods and Jaguars used the bases at Seeb and Muharrag in Bahrain, respectively.

Like other members of the Allied coalition, the RAF crews saw Desert Storm simply as a job to do—but that did not mean that the massive, often doom-laden media speculation on the outcome of 'their' war escaped them. Few could have failed to realise that their initial actions might have sparked off a protracted military campaign with terrible casualties on both sides of the line and peripheral action by nations sympathetic to Saddam Hussein. Never before had the preparations for a conflict involving the major powers been the subject of so much television and press scrutiny. Perhaps with the passing thought that war is too serious a business to have an army of ill-informed and doubtfully opinionated pundits decide the outcome beforehand, British crews briefed for a second round of RAF Desert Storm strikes in the early hours of the 17th.

A quartet of Tornado GR.1s armed with JP 233 queue up to refuel courtesy of a No. 55 Squadron Victor K.2, while a fifth Tornado, ZA459/EL, lacking the anti-runway weapon, keeps station to starboard. (14 Squadron, via BAe)

At 30 tonnes take-off weight, each Tornado needed a fuel top-off en route to its Iraqi target. VC 10s and Victors performed this service admirably, the former type doing the honours in this view, which shows two GR. 1s nuzzling into the drogues and a third machine, coded 'ER', awaiting its turn 'at the pump'. (14 Squadron, via BAe)

While few of the participating airmen underestimated the risk they ran, they knew they possessed a very important weapon in the JP 233. British crews had been perfecting the technique of airfield destruction since April 1985, when JP 233 was first issued to the RAF. Planners were convinced that the widespread damage that could be achieved with the weapon more than justified its demanding mode of delivery. The first strikes of Desert Storm appeared to bear this out, although it was realised that repeat attacks on bases with alerted defences would be necessary. Despite the decimation of their gun-laying radars, it was naive to expect the enemy flak crews to achieve absolutely nil results, as events were to prove.

By the time of the first combat sorties, the RAF had positioned VC 10 and Victor tankers to extend the Tornadoes' 480-mile combat range, and it became standard operational procedure for the strike aircraft to top off their tanks after climb-out to give them the maximum endurance for target strike and return. In respect of range, each GR.1 carried a pair of the 100 gal tanks developed for the GR.3.

The primary targets for the GR.1s were the most important of Iraq's 60 air bases, most of which were vulnerable to attack by aircraft making low-level (200 ft) runs dropping JP 233. Conventional 1,000 lb and 2,000 lb iron bombs were dropped from higher altitude, using loft or toss bombing delivery to minimize the risk to aircraft and crews.

Iraq's well reported threat to fight and to retaliate by attacking the cities of Israel with missiles, thereby widening the conflict and possibly forcing the Middle Eastern-based coalition support forces to choose between Arab and Jewish factions, and, at the very least, to cause a rift in the Alliance, gave the opening rounds of the war a highly-charged atmosphere. If the Allies could succeed in destroying much of the missile capability of Iraq before any such counter-offensive caused real damage in Israel, this threat would be mimimized.

Consequently, the initial Allied air sortie rate was very high. In the event it was not to be aerial bombs alone that blunted Saddam Hussein's missile offensive with the Russian Scud-B intermediate range ground to ground weapon, but the remarkable US Raytheon Patriot anti-missile-missile. Fortunately, the early anti-radar strikes succeeded in denying the enemy much of the accurate guidance necessary for SAMs to bring down attacking aircraft, and it was AAA (the guidance for which was also subject to intensive attack) that was to cause most of the losses among the strike forces.

As the sortie rate spiralled, the first Tornado aircrew casualties occurred. For the RAF these were to be far lower than had been feared, had Iraq flown the expectedly massive air interception of the first raids—but losses were nevertheless widely reported and deeply felt at unit level. The first GR.1 was lost on the second strike of 17 January, Flt Lts Adrian 'John' Nicholl and John Peters of 15 Squadron suffering the relatively rare occurrence of an AAA round hitting one of their Sidewinder AAMs and promptly exploding, ripping out sections of the wing as it did so. The crew ejected and both men landed safely in the desert to await rescue—or capture by the Iraqis. Unfortunately it was the latter, and very soon after the first Missing in Action (MIAs) had been reported, Nicholl and Peters appeared with other airmen on Iraqi television, having obviously been mistreated. The TV pictures and press photos taken from the transmissions were flashed around the world, causing a wave of sympathy for the PoWs and destroying any propaganda value Saddam Hussein might have gained from such a dubious exercise.

This initial loss was from a section of four Tornadoes based at Muhurraq which had been on a sortie to Shaibah, close to Basra, a target that gained some notoriety among the attacking crews. Aircraft of a third 17 January wave ran into trouble when four Tornadoes went to Shaibah and four to Ubaydah bin al Jarrah, all eight machines being armed with JP 233.

Having bombed Shaibah and escaped unscathed, while the Iraqi gunners were distracted by the pyrotechnics from the exploding oil refinery one mile north of the Tornadoes' track as well as the attention of USAF and Navy anti-radar strikes, the quartet of Tornadoes seemed to be in the clear. But suddenly the aircraft crewed by Wg Cdr Nigel Elsdon and Flt Lt Max Collier was seen to go down, presumably having taken a hit by AAA. Both men were killed.

Sorties continued into the early hours of 18 January, although the Tornado force stood down until darkness fell, bringing a slightly higher perceived threat from the defences which, once aroused by imminent air attack in their particular sector, responded with some spirit. The Iraqis also made use of their Euromissile Roland SAM, and it was one of these that nailed the third Tornado to be lost, the aircraft crewed by Flt Lts David Waddington and Robert Stuart. Trying desperately to out-manoeuvre the Roland, the crew felt the missile hit. Waddington was knocked unconscious as it exploded, and it was Stuart who activated the command ejection system. Flt Lts Pablo Mason and Mike Toft were flying wing on the downed Tornado, and witnessed the double ejection. Back at Muharraq they gave reporters every assurance that they believed the crew to have survived, and happily this proved to be the case.

The desert war took its toll on aircraft finish, as seen particularly well in this view of a Tornado GR.1 sporting the cartoon character 'Snoopy' on its nose. (617 Squadron, via BAe)

The sortie rate by Allied air forces quickly rose to some 2,000 per day. By 19 January a fourth Tornado, belonging to the Italian Air Force, had been lost. A fourth RAF aircraft was destroyed during the first weekend of the war when a GR.1 suffered a technical failure and crashed shortly after taking off from Tabuk. Both crewmen ejected safely.

During the early hours of 22 January another fatal loss was suffered by the RAF Tornado force. Eight Tabuk aircraft on a loft-bombing sortie on a radar at Ar Rutbah stirred up the now usual hornets' nest. A 16 Squadron crew, Sqn Ldrs Garry Lennox and Paul Weeks, were killed when their aircraft was shot down.

Loss number six occurred on 24 January, when Plt Off Simon Burgess and Sqn Ldr Bob Ankerson of 17 Squadron ejected when one of their 1,000 lb bombs exploded immediately after release, causing the aircraft to go out of control. Although the Iraqis deprived the Allies of any immediate news of their fate, both men were among the PoWs released after the ceasefire.

Crews reported that, although the sheer volume of AAA was almost bound to find targets among strike forces flying so low, much of the ground fire was inaccurate. The difference was that after the initial airfield strikes, the Iraqis had learned to fire horizontally rather than straight up. Pilots also reported that, as well as the larger-calibre guns, troops were firing at them, obviously hoping that a lucky hit from small arms would bring the attackers down.

Strangest of all was the almost total absence of Iraqi interceptors, although the few that had appeared in the early days of the conflict were promptly despatched or chased off by the highly effective CAP flown primarily by USAF F-15s and F-16s. In the first five days the Allies claimed 15 enemy aircraft shot down, including six MiG-29s, without question the IAF's best fighter.

It also became increasingly likely that, because the Allies had neutralised the primary enemy air bases, communications centres and some missile sites with minimal reaction from enemy aircraft, the main Iraqi offensive would be ground based. By the second week of the war, therefore, targets for air attacks increasingly became missile batteries, troop concentrations and tanks, although the good dispersal of these by the Iraqis made the job highly frustrating at times. Nevertheless, intelligence reports suggested that 16 out of 20 mobile missile launchers and all 30 fixed sites had been destroyed during the first phase.

Despite this general change of target emphasis, Iraq's airfields still had to be attacked to prevent repairs and any unexpected resurrection of the IAF—although, given the degree of surveillance, this was extremely unlikely. Airfield strikes did continue, however, and on 14 February the target for a Tornado force operating from Muharraq was Al Taqaddum. This time the defences were not smothered, and two of the notorious SA-2 Guideline SAMs struck ZD717. Rapid action enabled Flt Lt Rupert Clark to eject safely, but his navigator, Flt Lt Steve Hicks, did not make it and was killed. It was small comfort to other crews at Muharraq that this was to be the last Tornado crew fatality and aircraft loss of the Gulf War.

While Allied air force commanders were doubtless relieved that Iraqi aerial reaction had not materialised, the threat to Tel Aviv—and all that widespread destruction and casualties in the Israeli capital implied—remained very real. Iraq had built an inventory of surface-to-surface missiles around the Soviet SS-1C Scud-B and indigenous derivatives, including the 375-mile-range Al-Hussein and 560-mile Al-Abbas, both of which were capable of striking Tel Aviv.

The Scud family of surface-to-surface tactical missiles was developed as integral land-transportable systems with a range of 100 to 175 miles. Some of those supplied to Iraq were believed to have been deployed on local adaptations of the original Soviet MAZ-543 transporter-erector mobile launchers. The search for Scud launchers was intensified.

Capturing mobile missile launchers on video tape was the primary task of the six Tornado GR.1As equipped with Vinten 4000 horizon-to-horizon infrared linescan, the aperture for which is built into an under-nose housing. With the advantage of recording all useful information on videotape rather than film, the equipment needs no artificial illumination at night, when all Gulf missions were flown by the reconnaissance detachment. Each Tornado also has side-facing IR sensors, and relevant images are recorded by six video cameras which occupy the space for the twin 27 mm cannon in the standard aircraft.

That the Vinten images obtained in a total of 128 Gulf sorties were valuable is a tribute not only to the crews who flew them, but to the personnel of the Reconnaissance Intelligence Centre, who gleaned every last detail from tapes which often lacked definition. The entire system was new and virtually untested before the outbreak of hostilities, but 'Granby 2' modifications to improve imaging were made in time for the Tornado crews to overfly most areas of Iraqi territory where military installations and strategically important structures, such as bridges, were located.

Finding and pinpointing Scud launchers was deemed to be far and away the most important operational task, however, as Israel was not the only potential target for Iraqi missiles. There was considerable alarm when a number landed in the vicinity of Riyadh, the Saudi capital, beginning during the second week of the war. The biggest worry was what the missile warheads contained, the spectre of Iraq resorting to chemical and biological weapons persisting almost until the Allied victory. Nobody could be sure that Saddam Hussein would not resort to this form of warfare as the conventional conflict increasingly went against him. As a result, NCB protective clothing and gas masks were an encumberance that Allied forces, including aircrews, were obliged to live with while they were on the ground.

With Patriot batteries in position and Allied airpower operating continuously to hunt out and kill Iraqi radar, success against incoming Scuds was immediate. The balance of power remained firmly in Allied hands, and Iraq's most deadly card was, for the time being, trumped. Reports suggested that the aerial search for the elusive Iraqi launchers had met with less than 100 per cent success, despite the sophistication of the surveillance equipment employed on the task.

The remarkable BAe ALARM anti-radiation missile was just one of the new RAF weapons proven in action during the Gulf War. Two of them, the typical load, are seen here under the fuselage of a Tornado GR.1, which also carries drop tanks, a jammer and flare dispenser, the standard kit for most missions by this type. (BAe)

Fortunately the Patriot system, dormant for many years as a result of low funding, worked very well indeed, more than confirming the faith—not to mention vast quantities of dollars—pumped into this American anti-missile system.

A further system making its operational debut with the Gulf Tornado force was the BAe ALARM. A highly sophisticated anti-radiation missile, ALARM had only recently reached operational status, and even then had hardly been thoroughly tested in service. Number 20 Squadron took over the 'evaluation' task, which had suddenly become very much the real thing.

ALARM was to have been the responsibility of IX Squadron, but this unit's specialised involvement with the GR.1 bombing campaign led to a change, and No. 20 became the RAF's first 'ALARMists'. For the most part the unit flew missile-compatible aircraft previously issued to IX Squadron. These machines were fitted with the MIL STD 1553B digital databus, which enabled the crews to communicate with the missile, and four examples had night vision cockpit lighting. Other modifications enabled up to three ALARM rounds to be carried under the belly of the aircraft, thus clearing the wing pylons for drop tanks and the 'standard' Gulf chaff and jamming suite of pods.

Based at Tabuk, the ALARM Tornadoes were in action from the very beginning, two missile-equipped aircraft accompanying the first four GR.1s sent to attack Al Asad airfield on 16 January. Four out of six missiles were launched successfully from the optimum altitude of 200 ft, this being adequate to give the missile motor time to ignite before heading not for the ground, but upwards. At heights of up to 70,000 ft, ALARM loiters under a parachute and looks for a target in the form of a transmitting radar. When it finds one, the parachute is jettisoned and the missile dives.

As the war progressed, it became obvious that ALARM and other ARMs had more than done their job, if not by complete destruction, then at least by forcing Iraqi radar off the air whenever an Allied air raid was about to take place. By its very nature, ALARM generally lacked the spectacular results achieved by HARM and Shrike missiles—but ARMs are successful if they achieve radar shut-down merely by their presence. If the enemy dare not risk switching on, even for brief periods, his missile defences are rendered all but useless.

Few pilots and navigators appreciated this fact more than the men who flew the third type of RAF strike aircraft in the Gulf War, the Sepecat Jaguar. Trained, as are all strike squadrons, to attack from 'zero' altitude, the Jaguar Detachment of 12 aircraft quickly found that it could adopt operating heights of 10,000 ft and above. Normally this would have been little short of suicidal in hostile airspace bristling with AAA and SAM batteries, but such was the completeness of Allied suppression tactics that the Jaguars could carry out their missions in relative safety. The dozen aircraft flew a combined total of 617 sorties without loss, carrying out bombing, strafing, reconnaissance and support missions.

By the middle of the second week of the war the Allied command could confidently announce that tactical air superiority had been achieved, and that it was now able to deploy airpower against Saddam's forces before any large-scale ground battle for the liberation of Kuwait. Unpredictable to the end, the Iraqi dictator could still pull off some kind of military coup, but it became increasingly likely that he realised exactly what this would bring down on his country.

Hot cat. Jaguar GR.1A XZ113 banks away from the camera ship over the waters of the Gulf. To enable them to carry out their primary role more effectively and clear wing and fuselage stores stations for offensive weapons and fuel tanks, the Jaguars adopted overwing launchers for AIM-9L Sidewinder AAMs. No aircraft were lost in action. (BAe)

Despite the early Tornado losses and unavoidable peripheral battle damage, the Tornado GR.1 performed remarkably well in the demanding low-altitude-attack role. But there was little doubt as to the difficulty of rendering Iraqi airfields useless, primarily because of their sheer size. Some bases sprawled over areas as large as 5,000 acres, with 13,000 ft double runways, requiring exhausting and ultimately unproductive repeat strikes (due to the non-appearance of the IAF) to ensure that they remained inoperative.

That the Allied blitz had a great psychological as well as military impact on the Iraqi leadership was confirmed during the last week of January, when a large part of the air force assets were flown out to Iran. Under US surveillance, the exodus, which included first-line fighters and transports, was not interfered with. It was the beginning of an episode that enabled Hussein to emerge from the conflict with most of his airpower intact. It was a strange way to fight a war.

The defection of the IAF left control of the air almost totally in Allied hands. Apart from the continuing missile threat and some misgivings about the 'winability' of a full-scale ground conflict against fanatical, battle-hardened troops, the Gulf War's reality had largely turned the scare-mongering prewar disaster scenarios on their head.

Switching from the relatively unsophisticated strikes on airfields proper to the far more precise location and destruction of bridges and hardened aircraft shelters posed something of a problem for the Tornado force. The standard GR.1s lacked the necessary laser guidance for effective use of precision-guided munitions, and it was decided to deploy Buccaneers equipped with US Pave Spike designators to the Gulf.

The Buccaneers were to perform a valuable service just before and after the combat debut of Tornadoes equipped with the British Thermal Imaging and

RAF aircraft 'nose art' came back into vogue in a big way during the Gulf War, all three strike types being suitably adorned with (invariably) the female form, names, and sortie records. 'Armoured Charmer' graced ZC739/AC, one of the five TIALD-equipped machines used in action. (Brian Marsh)

Laser Designator (TIALD) pod. Six aircraft from No. 12 Squadron arrived during the week of 28 January. Armed with designators, AIM-9L launchers and flare and chaff dispensers, and wired to carry Paveway laser-guided bombs, the Buccs undertook a 'pathfinder' role for the Tornado force, as well as subsequently carrying out their own precision bombing strikes. Old airframes they may have been, but the strength built into the Buccaneers for their original carrier rôle stood them in good stead for an intensive series of airframe-buffeting low-level sorties against alerted defences.

TIALD was one of a number of Tornado weapons and systems that proved highly effective in combat, despite a hectic last-minute rush to get them to the Gulf in a satisfactory state of readiness. Similar in design to the US Pave Knife designator pod, except that it employs thermal-imaging rather than television for target designation, TIALD is day- and night-capable and incorporates in the nose of the pod a ball-shaped seeker head which rotates to provide lower hemisphere coverage.

In contrast, the Buccaneers could use Pave Spike only by day, but integration of TIALD Tornadoes and Buccs into strike cells enabled mixed formations to designate and destroy a variety of targets with a high degree of success. Once the target was 'coned' by laser beam, each aircraft type could maintain 'lock on' for the other, or carry out its own attack. The Buccaneer crews initially flew without bombs, but with the luxury of air superiority and the ever-present watch by the USAF's E-3 Sentry, plus radar detection and suppression by F-111s, F-4s and F-15s, the tough old machines made the most of their first—and almost certainly last—major war action.

Backed up by carpet-bombing Strategic Air Command B-52s, USAF and Navy air strikes and Kuwaiti, French and Italian sorties, the RAF continued to fly against a wide variety of targets, including some of the most difficult to destroy, namely bridges. There were 120 bridges in Iraqi hands in and around Kuwait, and it was necessary to knock out the most important of these to prevent enemy forces being moved up to the battlefields.

Among the options open to RAF strike forces was loft or toss bombing, which enabled aircraft to take out targets while remaining well out of range of enemy defences. A great deal depended on the type of target. For example, it was unproductive to use smart bombs against 'soft' targets and conventional weapons against reinforced concrete. The trick was to integrate the Allied air forces so that mutal support could be given, with the right electronic backup and weapons being deployed against key targets for the utmost economy in terms of crew casualties and aircraft losses.

When the Iraqi Army finally decided to move up to front-line positions, it was subjected to an intensive round-the-clock series of air strikes that disrupted anything the enemy tried to achieve. They came up against US and Allied armour and broke up into isolated and small-scale skirmishes in which the attackers invariably took casualties in men and equipment. Overall, it was more than obvious that Saddam Hussein's bid to hold on to Kuwait was a lost cause.

It came as no surprise to Allied commanders that the Iraqis were detected moving *en masse* in and around Kuwaiti territory, and although, on the face of it, they maintained the initiative as to where and when to fight, that was little more than an illusion. Command of the air handed this almost totally to the Allies.

As Saddam's military strategy was proved wanting, there were renewed fears that he would resort to chemical weapons to help restore the lost initiative. There was no room for complacency on the part of the air force commanders. And the Scud missile threat, though reduced, had not been entirely eliminated by early February. Overall, though, the war had gone well for the coalition, with Iraq's conventional forces being more than contained.

On 3/4 February the Allied air forces' sortie rate was as high as ever, at some 2,500. The total included 20 or so 'package missions' aimed specifically at neutralising the Republican Guard, Iraq's crack first-line force. The Guard was consequently pounded wherever its positions were located. The Iraqis were rapidly being bottled up in Kuwait city and surrounding areas, Allied ground forces having planned an armoured pincer movement to disastrously split the enemy. Airpower assets were now deployed against tactical targets and in a direct battlefield support role, helicopter gunships and A-10 tank busters (the latter type making its combat debut) providing excellent air cover for friendly armour and infantry.

The difficult technique of hitting bridges with high explosive without plastering civilian dwellings grouped closely around their approaches was demonstrated when the 600 yd long al-Nasir bridge spanning the Euphrates at

Tabuk's Tornadoes sported one of the oldest of aircraft combat markings, the sharkmouth. 'MiG Eater' was the name applied to ZA447/EA, along with a cartoon shark and an impressive scoreboard. It includes one MiG-29 destroyed on the ground, and 'iron' and guided bomb sorties. (Brian Marsh)

al-Nasiriyeh city, in southern Iraq, was hit on 4 February. Eyewitnesses reported that, when the air strike took place at 15:00 hr, at least four bombs hit the target. Four of the bridge spans were hit and a pier was partially destroyed at the eastern end of the structure, dropping two spans into the river. Owing to the destruction of other bridges, the al-Nasier was carrying abnormally high civilian

Many Tornadoes took their names from their single or double letter codes, as shown by ZD890/AJ 'Amanda Jane'. (Brian Marsh)

traffic at the time of the attack, and a number of people were killed. Ironically, the bridge had been built by British engineers in the mid-1950s.

Allied aircraft also successfully attacked the Expressway bridge at Nasiriyeh, a city lying 250 miles south of Baghdad. A complete span was wrecked and some civilian houses adjacent to one end of the bridge, fortunately unoccupied, were hit by stray bombs. Among the 72 successful TIALD strikes carried out by the Tornado force was the 17 February attack on the As Samawah rail bridge across the Euphrates.

With Iraqi troops now deserting in substantial numbers to swell PoW compounds, Allied air attacks were increasingly being unwittingly directed against civilian rather than military traffic, refugees from the fighting who were attempting to leave areas likely to be attacked. But the pressure could not be slackened while the Iraqi Army existed as a cohesive force.

Four of the twelve bridges over the Tigris identified as primary targets had been put out of action by 13 February, the Allied intention being to divide and isolate Baghdad into western and eastern sectors, cutting all the bridges if possible. Allied pilots were also required to knock out pontoon bridges thrown across rivers when the more permanent structures were cut or destroyed. These temporary crossing points were quickly established along the main supply routes into Kuwait.

It was not the first time that civilian casualties had been caused by mistake— or that non-combatants had deliberately been placed in harm's way—and the Iraqi regime knew full well the propaganda value of publicity given to the 'deliberate and indiscriminate' bombing of civilians. There were numerous accusations that Allied airmen had acted irresponsibly during the Gulf War, but few could really be sure that Iraq had not deliberately tried to disguise military installations with a civilian façade to avoid attack.

By mid-February the sortie rate against Baghdad had dropped to around 150–200 per day, and pilots found that they were being briefed for targets against which they had already flown five or six times. Things came to a head after the headlined Baghdad bunker attack on 13 February, in which hundreds of people died. Clearly some rethinking of Allied strategy was necessary, both to avoid a similar incident and to prevent wasteful repeat raids on targets that were beyond immediate repair.

On 13 February the Tornadoes were out again after bridges over the Euphrates. During a strike on the bridge of Soluja one laser-guided bomb missed its target and promptly veered off to land in the town of Fallouja. This was not in any way a deliberate attack on a civilian target, but the action of a bomb apparently freed of its laser 'basket'. In this instance the RAF crews aimed for the centre of the bridge span, rather than placing their bombs at each end of the structure, as was more usual practice. This was done to minimise casualties, as the town itself was close to the bridge approaches. At least one bomb hit the bridge, but the 'wild' bomb landed some 800 yd off target, having either missed the funnel of refracted light centred on the target, or through a fault in the guide vanes. The RAF was baffled by the incident, as it is rare for guided bombs to react in such a way.

Being able to use laser guided bombs meant that individual hangars, shelters and other buildings on Iraqi airfields could be taken out with a success rate of

Back in the UK, many of the Gulf War Tornadoes could be seen at summer air shows. This GR.1, ZD810/AA, poses with an F.3 at Alconbury in front of a hardened aircraft shelter—the very kind of structure that Tornadoes successfully destroyed in Iraq. (Brian Marsh)

Another Tabuk 'tiger' was ZA465/FK 'Foxy Killer'. (Brian Marsh)

80 per cent or higher. Therefore, TIALD Tornadoes and Pave Way Buccaneers were briefed to return to the airfields at Al Asad, Habbaniyah, Jalibah Southeast, Mudaysis and Tallil, among many others.

By 15 February, the stream of Allied communiques included some of the statistics of battle: 1,300 tanks, 600 AFVs and 1,100 artillery pieces destroyed or disabled by air attack in what was now designated as the KTO—Kuwait Theatre of Operations. In addition, half of Iraq's hardened aircraft shelters had been rendered unusable or were considered to have been destroyed. Up to 70,000 sorties had been flown up to that date, 2,800 in the previous 24 hours. Of these, 800 were against targets in Kuwait, and the remainder on positions occupied by the Republican Guard.

Disruption of the supply lines had been widely achieved, and the enemy was obliged to reduce road transportation drastically, trucks and tankers plying the highways being considered fair game for Allied fighter-bombers. The Iraqi regime was also widely reported to have been executing Kuwaiti civilians—and individual troops and commanders for lacking fighting spirit.

With more and more prisoners coming over to the Allied side, the ground war finally opened with a massive artillery bombardment of Iraqi positions. During the weekend of 23/24 February the Allies finally thrust into Kuwait, pushing the Iraqis back. Some resistance was apparent as night fell on G-Day, the first day of the invasion, but Allied casualties remained remarkably light. Demoralised by the continuing bombing, the Iraqis appeared to have no effective counter to the armoured penetrations, backed by helicopter troop lifts and strafing by A-10s and helicopter gunships.

By advancing on a broad front, the coalition kept the enemy guessing as to which was the main thrust and which were have been feints to draw his fire. With no air cover, those Iraqi units caught in the open suffered grievously and more men surrendered, many of them stating that they had been threatened with torture or death if they did not commit what amounted to suicide by facing overwhelming Allied might. Few chose that path.

Neither did the Iraqis appear keen to deploy their substantial battlefield support assets along sound tactical lines. There appeared to be little evidence of an overall battle plan. The RAF strike continued to maintain the air umbrella, the rapid advance now presenting a challenge to mission planning. Friendly forces were now very much on the battlefield, a fact that was to lead to the death of both British and American troops from friendly air attacks.

By 27 February the key to the Allied ground offensive—indeed the key to victory in the entire Gulf War—was announced. Allied troops entered Kuwait City, virtually without a fight. Combat did, of course, occur; numerous small-scale skirmishes caused casualties on both sides, but in general the liberation of Kuwait was completed in short order without heavy Allied losses in men or equipment.

Having thrust eastwards and reached a point west of Basra, US forces engaged some 200 Iraqi tanks dug into defensive positions—but these localised firefights were to be the last of the conflict. It fell to the US 24th Mechanised Infantry division to finish the ground war, Allied forces having occupied the entire southwestern corner of Iraq and retaken all Saudi Arabian territory. The British First Armoured Division experienced a rapid turn-around of duty, as its men and tanks were soon deployed to cover Iraqi movements out of the beleaguered and badly damaged city. The formal ceasefire to end hostilities was signed at 08:00 hr local time on 28 February. It was reliably stated that, by that time, the Iraqis had one and a half divisions still capable of putting up a fight.

To win a decisive victory, the Allies flew some 110,000 sorties and lost a total of 42 aircraft in combat plus 33 in accidents. Overall, the combat loss rate was less than one tenth of one per cent. The highest statistical loss ratio was suffered by the Tornado GR.1—six aircraft in nearly 1,650 sorties, although, at only just over one third of one per cent, this figure was equally remarkable and the best returned by any air force in any previous high-intensity war.

In general terms the Gulf War was a complete victory for the Allied coalition. While the coalition was undeniably strong, it was not overwhelmingly so, particularly on the ground. Properly used, Saddam Hussein's armoured forces alone could have prolonged the fight and made Allied victory far more costly. It was also one of the few occasions in modern war where airpower supported other forces so well that the taking of enemy territory was little more than a formality. Desert Storm lasted a total of 42 days, from 17 January to 28 February.

That the enemy could have also made this effort highly costly does not in any way detract from the achievement of Allied airmen. They knew that well enough, and indeed were probably surprised that the loss of life was very low, considering the intensive effort involved. Perhaps the war, which came at a time when the greatest perceived threat to the peace of the world was finally being

An ALARM-carrying Tornado GR.1 over Germany, Laarbruch being home for No. 20 Squadron. After the conflict, many Tornadoes, including ZA411/GY, retained the Gulf colour scheme. (BAe)

dismantled in Eastern Europe and the Soviet Union, was a timely lesson, pointing to a future need for nations to act not alone, but as a combined force to meet any threat to peace wherever it may occur. In and around the Gulf battleground, large-scale suffering and deprivation was to bring a grim aftermath to the fighting, and it remains to be seen whether a lasting peace and political stability can eventually be achieved throughout the Middle East without resort to force of arms.

RAF Tornadoes lost in combat and accidents

Crew	Unit	Date	Aircraft	Fate
Flt Lt Adrian Nicholl	No. 15	16 Jan	ZD791/BG	PoW
Flt Lt John Peters	No. 15			PoW
Wg Cdr Nigel Elsdon	No. 27	17 Jan	ZA392/EK	KIA
Flt Lt Max Collier	No. 27			KIA
Flt Lt David Waddington	No. 27	19 Jan	ZA396/GE	PoW
Flt Lt Robert Stuart	No. 27			PoW
Sqn Ldr Peter Battson	No. 20	20 Jan	ZD893/AG	Ej
Wg Cdr Mike Heath	No. 20			Ej
Sqn Ldr Garry Lennox	No. 16	22 Jan	ZA467/FF	KIA
Sqn Ldr Paul Weeks	No. 16			KIA
Sqn Ldr Bob Ankerson	No. 17	24 Jan	ZA403/CO	PoW
Pet Off Simon Burgess	No. 17			PoW
Flt Lt Rupert Clark	No. 15	14 Feb	ZD717/CD	PoW
Flt Lt Steve Hicks	No. 15			KIA

NB: In addition, ZA466/FH and ZD718/BH were destroyed on training flights in the Gulf area before the conflict began.

Index